THE ENGLISH OF CHAUCER
and his contemporaries

AUP Titles of related interest

A LINGUISTIC ATLAS OF LATE MEDIAEVAL ENGLISH
Angus McIntosh, M L Samuels, Michael Benskin with the assistance of Margaret Laing and Keith Williamson

GUIDE TO A LINGUISTIC ATLAS OF LATE MEDIAEVAL ENGLISH

MIDDLE ENGLISH DIALECTOLOGY
essays on some principles and problems
by Angus McIntosh, M L Samuels, Margaret Laing and Keith Williamson, edited and introduced by Margaret Laing

WALTER BOWER'S SCOTICHRONICON
in nine volumes
original Latin with English translation
Volume Two *edited John and Winifred MacQueen*
Volume Eight *edited D E R Watt*

Scottish Text Society Texts
THE MEROURE OF WYSSDOME by Johannes de Irlandia, II
edited Matthew P MacDiarmid
THE WORKS OF ALLAN RAMSAY, IV, V AND VI
ANDREW CRAWFORD'S COLLECTION OF BALLADS AND SONGS, I
edited E B Lyle
JAMES WATSON'S CHOICE COLLECTION, I
edited Harriet Harvey Wood
THE COMPLAYNT OF SCOTLAND
edited A M Stewart
BARBOUR'S BRUCE, I, II and III
edited Matthew P McDiarmid and James A C Stevenson
THE MINOR PROSE OF JAMES VI AND I
edited James Craigie
THE BUIK OF KING ALEXANDER THE CONQUEROR, II and III
edited J Cartwright

THE ENGLISH OF CHAUCER
and his contemporaries

Essays by M L SAMUELS
and J J SMITH

edited by J J SMITH

ABERDEEN UNIVERSITY PRESS

First published 1988
Aberdeen University Press
A member of the Pergamon Group

British Library Cataloguing in Publication Data

Samuels, Michael
The English of Chaucer and his contemporaries.
1. English language, 1066–1400
I. Title II. Smith, J J (Jeremy J)
427'.02

ISBN 0-08-036403-9

PRINTED IN GREAT BRITAIN
THE UNIVERSITY PRESS
ABERDEEN

CONTENTS

EDITORIAL PREFACE

In preparing these essays for publication—in most cases, for republication—editorial intervention has been kept to the minimum. The manner of citation has been harmonised and some references to new work have been added. No attempt has been made to remove portions of argument repeated from essay to essay; it is felt that any repetition should clarify rather than obscure the arguments presented.

Acknowledgements are due to the following editors and publishers for allowing material already printed to be republished here:

> the Editors, *Notes and Queries*, and Oxford University Press for 'Chaucerian final *-e*'; the Editors, *Neuphilologische Mitteilungen* for 'The language of Gower'; Professors D Gray and E G Stanley, and Oxford University Press, for 'Chaucer's Spelling'; the Editor, *Studies in the Age of Chaucer*, and the New Chaucer Society for 'The Scribe of the Hengwrt and Ellesmere Manuscripts of the *Canterbury Tales*'; the Editors, *Medium Ævum*, and B H Blackwell for 'Langland's Dialect'.

In those articles already published, acknowledgement was made to the help of Professor Michael Benskin, Dr Ian Doyle, Dr José Gómez Soliño, Dr Malcolm Parkes and Professor Arthur Sandved; to this list must now be added Mr Jeremy Griffiths, Ms Kate Harris, Professor Charles Owen, Professor Derek Pearsall and Dr Jane Roberts. The orientation of this book derives from the work of the Middle English Dialect Project (now the Gayre Institute, University of Edinburgh), and the editor especially wishes to thank the Project's founder, Professor Angus McIntosh, and his associate Dr Margaret Laing for their essential help, criticism and encouragement in producing this book. The editor is further indebted to Ms Elaine Higgleton and Mr John Smith for advice and support, and to his colleagues at Glasgow University for co-operating in a system of sabbatical leave which made it possible. Mr Colin MacLean and Miss Marjorie Leith of Aberdeen University Press have been both patient and helpful.

Most of the articles in this book are by Professor Michael Samuels, and all—including the Introduction—bear the imprint of his special combination of intellectual insight, attention to detail and argument, and careful and scholarly supervision. It so happens that the publication of this volume marks, coincidentally, his impending retirement as Professor of English Language at Glasgow University, an appointment he had held with distinction since 1959. Michael abhors an excess of personal compliment; for this reason, the editor wishes simply to record his gratitude for being allowed to treat his work in this way, and to hope that he may find some pleasure in seeing it assembled here.

Responsibility for the authorship of the individual chapters is indicated in the table of contents. The Indices and Bibliography were compiled by the editor.

1 INTRODUCTION

J J SMITH

I

Of late, students of Middle English have placed considerable emphasis on the activity of scribes as a positive source of information for the understanding of the literature of the period. Scholars are now aware of the 'virtues of bad texts',[1] how the Middle Ages saw the activities of *auctor* and *scriptor* as being simply two 'ways of making a book'.[2] As Margaret Laing has put it most recently, 'close examination of scribal behaviour, whether it be script, spelling, or choice and ordering of material provides insight into the way literary texts were received, understood and disseminated.'[3]

Although these interests have developed comparatively recently, it so happens that a body of evidence of close relevance to them had been in process of collection for over thirty years previously, and came to fruition with the publication, in 1986, of *A Linguistic Atlas of Late Mediaeval English* (hence *LALME*,[4] and it is from the making of *LALME* that the group of essays presented here derives. It is designed to complement the collection of papers by Angus McIntosh, Michael Samuels and Margaret Laing, *Middle English Dialectology: essays on some principles and problems*.[5] The present book differs from that volume in that the latter covers wider ground, including discussion of the theoretical and dialectological underpinning of the approach to the study of Middle English used here, and for which reference should also be made to *LALME*.[6] This volume further illustrates the approach outlined in those places, but is primarily focused on specific Middle English authors: Chaucer, Langland and Gower. Together the two collections of essays constitute a prolegomenon to a whole field of research. They show that the publication of *LALME* has been a landmark not just for the historical linguist; in Laing's words, the 'studies of palaeographer, dialectologist, textual critic, and literary historian can and should be complementary'.[7]

What follows here is a brief introduction to the theoretical and historical orientation of these essays, but it should be emphasised that such a sketch cannot be a substitute for the works already referred to above.

II

A central problem addressed in these essays is: how is the original language (i.e., in the first instance, the spelling) of a Middle English author to be established? Since readers interested in Chaucer, Langland and Gower may not be acquainted with certain of the relevant facts about Middle English that must underlie any approach to this question, a brief historical outline is given here.

The key to understanding Middle English is an understanding of linguistic variation; as Barbara Strang put it, '[Middle English] is, *par excellence*, the dialectal phase of English, in the sense that while dialects have been spoken at all periods, it was in [the Middle English period] that divergent local usage was normally indicated in writing'.[8] This diversity arose because of the social prestige of the written language during the mediaeval period. After the Norman Conquest, Latin became widespread as the language of record and of 'serious' literature, whereas the native language of the new rulers was Norman French. English became a debased vernacular, generally unsuited for discourse on matters of fundamental importance.[9] As a result, no variety of English possessed any special prestige and, when English *was* written, it reflected the natural dialectal variation of the spoken medium more closely than ever since. Written variation manifested itself not only in the reflection of dialect differences found in speech (e.g. *drives* vs. *driveth*), but also in local orthographic traditions without significance for the spoken language (e.g. *it* vs. *itt*); and each scribe's spelling-system consisted of an idiosyncratic selection from both types of variation. A scribe's written language could even contain variable forms for the same item.[10] This state of affairs gradually changed during the Middle Ages, but it was not until after 1430 that English began to be used regularly for official purposes, and 'Chancery English' became available as a unifying model.[11] Even the arrival of printing in England in 1475 did not prevent personal spelling from remaining highly individual until well into the sixteenth century.[12]

The result of this situation is that, when not copying (i.e. 'naturally'), a writer's own usage is virtually a unique collection of habits which reflected his own personal history and background. When copying, however, a scribe's reaction to his exemplar can be very complex; and, since almost all mediaeval English texts are transmitted to us through scribal copies,[13] it is important to understand these complexities if the original language of literary works is to be reconstructed. *Literatim*-copies, reproducing the spellings of an exemplar letter-by-letter, are not unknown in the fourteenth century,[14] and authorial spellings can be transmitted in that way. However, it was more usual for scribes either to translate into their own 'natural' dialect or to use a mixture of their own forms and those of their exemplar, wiping out or obscuring the authorial language in the process.[15]

The habits of *literatim*-scribes and complete 'translators' are comparatively straightforward, but the complexities involved in 'partial translation' are considerable; they have been exhaustively discussed elsewhere, notably in *LALME*.[16] In brief, one group of 'partial translators' consists of copyists who are largely translators, but who occasionally reproduce forms from their exemplars which are not part of their own 'natural' usage. Such forms are termed 'relicts' or 'relict forms'. At the other end of the spectrum, there are scribes who attempt *literatim*-copying, but who occasionally let slip their 'natural' usage, thereby betraying their dialectal origins. Yet other scribes vary in the use of relict and their own forms; this can be without any motivation obvious to us, or as part of a pattern of 'progressive translation' (whereby the copyist imposes his own usage gradually on that of his exemplar as copying proceeds), or even as 'progressive *literatim*-copying' (whereby the scribe abandons his own usage for that of his exemplar during the progress of his stint).[17] Complications to this picture include: (a) 'constrained' behaviour, in which a scribe departs from his normal habit of using two variables in a given proportion, and instead uses only one of them because of its coincidental presence in his exemplar;[18] and (b) towards the end of the period, scribal behaviour showing the impact of incipient standardisation.[19]

III

Even though these essays began life as independent investigations into problems concerning scribal copying and the reconstruction of authorial practices, they are all linked by a single theme, viz. that it is possible to detect meaningful patterns of scribal behaviour, but that scribes react variously to the various pressures which bear upon them. If history is the essence of innumerable biographies, then the history of later Middle English is the sum of innumerable scribal choices. For this reason it is essential to study each set of scribal practices individually for, although some scribes may be found to show similar patterns of behaviour, there are always others regarding whom such an approach would be misleading. Scribal behaviour can be seen as like much other human behaviour: unpredictable and multifarious, even though organised around certain governing principles and not random.

Each of the chapters of this book, therefore, proceeds from a similar theoretical orientation, but the precise methods employed in the solution of each problem vary considerably according to the nature of each author's text and its transmission. Thus, in chapter 2, the method used is the fairly generalised one of assembling evidence for a linguistic feature—the use of 'final *-e*'—observed in a wide variety of scribes which can then be used to cast light on Chaucer's metrical practice.

By contrast, chapter 3 attempts to explain why Gower's language is a consistent, non-random mixture of two dialects, each vouched for as authorial by the metre, and the solution to this problem itself establishes the authorial authenticity of the language of the Fairfax and Stafford manuscripts of the *Confessio Amantis*. This provides the basis for the study of the behaviour of the two earliest Chaucerian scribes in chapters 4 to 6. In chapter 4, by observing the behaviour of these scribes when copying non-Chaucerian (including Gowerian) exemplars, it is shown that Chaucer's own spellings were not those used by the Hengwrt/Ellesmere scribe, but must have closely resembled, if not completely matched, those found in the *Equatorie of the Planetis*.

Crucial to the study of scribal behaviour is comparison of works by the same scribe copying from different exemplars in different manuscript-traditions. In chapter 4, the key to identifying potentially Chaucerian—as opposed to scribal—forms rests on the assumption, strongly backed by palaeographical evidence,[20] that the same scribe copied the Hengwrt and Ellesmere manuscripts of the *Canterbury Tales*, part of the Trinity Cambridge *Confessio Amantis* and the 'Cecil Fragment' of *Troilus and Criseyde*, and that a second scribe copied MSS of *Piers Plowman*, Trevisa, the *Canterbury Tales* and Gower. These identities, however, have been questioned; and it is, of course, a fact that, without an explicit scribal colophon to prove it in each case, palaeographical evidence can never do any more than establish high probabilities of identity of hand, not certainties.[21] Something nearer to proof can come only from a combination of the palaeographical evidence and study of the linguistic behaviour of the scribe.[22] It is this necessary and complementary evidence that is set out in chapters 5 and 6.

The *Piers Plowman* manuscripts, again, contrast with those of Chaucer and Gower in that they contain, when considered overall, no clear indications of the archetypal language. Here, the only available starting-point is the dialectal evidence of the alliterations which formed a key element in Langland's metrical practice. In chapter 7 it is shown how this can be used to throw light on the archetypal language and its surviving representation in the 'B' and 'C' traditions of the poem.

The transmission of Middle English literary texts during the fifteenth century is related to the processes of standardisation of the written medium, and it is with this topic that chapters 8 and 9 are engaged. Chapter 8 deals with the changing practices of copyists in the fifteenth century, especially as a result of standardisation, while chapter 9 examines the way in which the pressures of standardisation and textual tradition interrelate in the language of the manuscripts of Gower's *Confessio Amantis*. Chapter 9 also investigates the usefulness of orthographic study for the practice of textual criticism, specifically with reference to the transmission of this poem.

A salient feature of all the chapters discussed above is that the language of copyists is as interesting as the language of authors. These studies are concerned with manuscripts containing the works of major Middle English poets—Chaucer, Gower, Langland—but sight is not lost of the humbler users of the language who have transmitted the poetry of these great men down to us. John Dryden wrote that 'from Chaucer the Purity of the English Tongue began';[23] in fact, Walter Raleigh was more to the point when he wrote that 'no poet makes his own language'.[24] Chaucer and his contemporaries, including his scribes, formed a linguistic community; and to understand a poet's use of language it is necessary to understand the linguistic milieu within which he worked.

NOTES

1 See K Harris, 'John Gower's *Confessio Amantis*: the virtues of bad texts', in D A Pearsall ed., *Manuscripts and Readers in Fifteenth-Century England*, Brewer: Cambridge, 1983, 27–40, and references there cited.

2 The phrase is St Bonaventure's (*modus faciendi librum*). See J A Burrow, *Mediaeval Writers and their Work*, OUP: Oxford, 1982, pp.29–30 and reference there cited.
3 M Laing, 'Dialectal analysis and linguistically composite texts in Middle English', *Speculum* 63, 1988, 83–103, p.83 (repr in *Middle English Dialectology*, chapter 13).
4 See Bibliography under *LALME*. For a history of the Middle English Dialect Project (now the Gayre Institute for Mediaeval English and Scottish Dialectology, Edinburgh University), from which *LALME* derives, see M Benskin, 'The Middle English Dialect Atlas', in M Benskin and M L Samuels eds, *So meny people longages and tonges: philological essays in Scots and mediaeval English presented to Angus McIntosh*, MEDP: Edinburgh, 1981, xxvii–xli.
5 See Bibliography under *Middle English Dialectology*.
6 See *LALME*, General Introduction to Vol I.
7 Laing, 'Dialectal analysis', p.83.
8 B M H Strang, *A History of English*, Methuen: London, 1970, p.224.
9 On the relationship between Latin, French and English in England during the Old and Middle English periods, see G Bourcier and C Clark, *An Introduction to the History of the English Language*, Thornes: Cheltenham, 1981, especially chapters 9 and 14. A more detailed account appears in M T Clanchy, *From Memory to Written Record*, Arnold: London, 1979, esp. chapter 6. See also E G Stanley ed., *The Owl and the Nightingale*, 2nd edn., MUP: Manchester, 1972, p.25.
10 Cf. variation in the spoken language, e.g. [ˈaɪðə] beside [ˈiðə] for 'EITHER' in the idiolects of many modern English speakers. On such variation, see esp. chapter 6 below.
11 On the emergence of standard written English, see *LALME*, Vol I, p.27 and references there cited; also M L Samuels, 'Some applications of Middle English dialectology', *English Studies* 44, 1963, 81–94 (repr in *Middle English Dialectology*, chapter 5).
12 See chapter 8 below.
13 Mediaeval English texts that survive in the handwriting of their authors are very rare, though not unknown, e.g. the *Ormulum*, Dan Michel's *Ayenbite of Inwyt*, certain MSS of Hoccleve's poetry (Huntington Cal., HM 111 and HM 744; Durham, University Library, MS Cosin V.III.9) and, perhaps, *The Equatorie of the Planetis*.
14 A good example in the Gower tradition is BL Harley 3869, a letter-by-letter copy of the Fairfax MS. See p.109 below.
15 This scribal typology was first distinguished by Angus McIntosh, 'Word geography in the lexicography of mediaeval English', *Annals of the New York Academy of Sciences* 211, 1973, 55–66, esp. p.61 (repr in *Middle English Dialectology*, chapter 7).
16 *LALME*, Vol I, esp. pp.12–23; see also pp.29–33. This largely reproduces M Benskin and M Laing, 'Translations and *Mischsprachen* in Middle English Manuscripts', in Benskin and Samuels, *So meny people*, 55–106.
17 'Progressive *literatim*-copying' has, perhaps, been rather neglected; see J J Smith, *Studies in the language of some manuscripts of Gower's Confessio Amantis*, Diss. PhD, Glasgow, 1985, chapter 4 *passim*.
18 A good example of 'constraint' is 'Scribe B's' use of *þ* and *th* (see chapters 4–6 below, and references there cited). Scribe B uses *th* when copying Chaucer, *þ* when copying Gower, and *th* once more when reverting to Chaucer. This has been considered unlikely (see R V Ramsey, 'Palaeography and scribes of shared training', *Studies in the Age of Chaucer* 8, 107–44, pp.125–6), but the presence of *þ* in the archetypal Gowerian language (cf. chapter 3 below) and the advancing form *th* in the archetypal Chaucerian language as well as in the (possible) Chaucerian holograph *Equatorie of the Planetis* (cf. chapter 4 below) accounts for the phenomenon.

19 See chapter 8 below.
20 See A I Doyle and M B Parkes, 'The production of copies of the *Canterbury Tales* and the *Confessio Amantis* in the early fifteenth century', in M B Parkes and A G Watson eds, *Mediaeval Scribes, Manuscripts and Libraries: essays presented to N R Ker*, Scolar Press: London, 1978, 163–210.
21 See A McIntosh, 'Scribal profiles from Middle English texts', *Neuphilologische Mitteilungen* 76, 1975, 218–35, p.220 (repr in *Middle English Dialectology*, chapter 3).
22 See A McIntosh, 'Towards an inventory of Middle English scribes', *Neuphilologische Mitteilungen* 75, 1974, 602–24 (repr in *Middle English Dialectology*, chapter 4); also McIntosh, 'Scribal profiles'.
23 Preface to the *Fables* (1700), quoted in J A Burrow ed., *Penguin Critical Anthologies: Geoffrey Chaucer*, Penguin: Harmondsworth, 1969, p.60.
24 'On Chaucer' (1926), quoted in Burrow, *Chaucer*, p.131.

2 CHAUCERIAN FINAL '-E'

M L Samuels

The view that Chaucer did not write in decasyllables has been repeated with such monotonous regularity during recent decades that there is some danger that it may eventually be believed. It formed the basis of J G Southworth's arguments in 1947, 1949, 1954 and 1962; and, only recently, it has appeared again as part of a somewhat different hypothesis advanced by I Robinson.[1] In his book, Mr Robinson represents present-day scholars of Middle English as hiding behind metaphor, and a reviewer of his book apparently accepts such comments as justified when he writes: 'he leans with perfect justice on the uncertainty of philological experts about this feature of our language [sc. final *-e*] in Chaucer's day.'[2] It thus appears that the onus of proof is being placed on the linguist, and, since neither Middle English studies nor linguistics are subjects that are wholly static, it may be of more than passing interest to show that there is a clear answer that can be given.

But first it should be noted that doubts about the traditional view appear to rest on a misunderstanding of the evidence presented in the past, since the figures for *-e* in all functions have usually been combined. Such blanket figures naturally look less conclusive than the separate ones would; they give the misleading impression that the question is open to debate, and mask the central point (one which rightly seemed conclusive to philologists earlier in the century): the distribution of adjectival forms which is required by a regular syllabic metre. If we discount all cases of elision (as we are certainly entitled to do),[3] the residue presents a distribution which is practically a mirror-image of the grammatical distinctions in Old English adjectives. Those derived from Germanic *-ja*-stems, like *dear*, *sweet*, *green*, demand *-e* throughout; others, like *good* or *old*, demand *-e* in the plural only of the strong declension, but in both singular and plural in the weak declension, so that there is a consistent distinction, even in consecutive lines, between *an old man*, with *man* in the metrical thesis, and *this olde man*, with arsis on *man* (for consecutive examples, see *Canterbury Tales*, C 713–4, 720, 740, 743, 745). Even special details, such as *-e* with adjectives preceding proper names and vocatives (cf. *olde cherl*, ibid., C 750) have their parallels in Old English, and should be regarded, not as 'exceptions', but as further confirming the authenticity of the distribution as grammmatical. Real exceptions are statistically few, and can in any case be described in grammatical terms appropriate to Middle (not Old) English.

Weak and strong adjectives

This traditional case is assailed mainly on the following grounds: that so little is known of the London dialect in the fourteenth century, and of the exact process of the loss of *-e*, that the argument must be held to be circular; that the scribal evidence for *-e* is invalid, since it could be due merely to scribal conservatism, not to spoken usage; and that, if grammatical rules are the reason for the alternation of forms in the adjective, then rules of exactly the same kind ought to apply to nouns and verbs.

The above arguments may be answered as follows. Firstly, they ignore a considerable body of evidence that is available from elsewhere in Middle English. There are a large number of primarily non-Chaucerian manuscripts, in both prose and verse, whose scribes make the same distinctions as we postulate for Chaucer's adjectives; these manuscripts were copied, by the process of scribal 'translation' common at the time,[4] in the dialects of a large area of the south-east and the SE Midlands, and date not only from Chaucer's time but also from the early fifteenth century. I list here a representative selection of twenty-five examples:[5]

Bodl Bodley 840, Douce 126 and 141, e Musaeo 116, Rawlinson C.57, Tanner 17.
Brasenose Oxford 9.
BL Harley 565, 2372 and 2387, Sloane 73 (ff.95–146) and 2593.
Caius, Cambridge 386.
CUL Dd.xii.69, Ff.v.40, and Addl 2380.
Corpus Christi, Cambridge 282 and 434.
Dulwich Coll 24.
Lambeth Palace 392.
Library of Congress 4 (ff. 1–40)
St John's, Cambridge 28 (B.6)[6] and 71 (C.21).
St John's, Oxford 138
University Coll, Oxford 142

Now, one can have a scribal tradition which imposes, say, the spelling *first* rather than *ferst* or *furst* irrespective of the scribe's pronunciation, and one might even imagine a tradition which prescribed rules for *first* in the singular of strong adjectives but *firste* in the plural. But a tradition which could have instructed Middle English scribes in the details of the Germanic weak adjective is beyond the bounds of reasonable surmise; if scribes distinguish between (1) the form *old* when it stands after 'an', 'any', 'each', 'every', 'some', 'is', 'was', etc and (2) the form *olde* after 'the', 'this', 'that', 'my', 'thy', 'his', 'her', 'our', 'your', 'their' (and when vocative), then this can represent nothing other than a corresponding distinction in contemporary speech. That this distribution of *-e* is the scribes' own (not that of their originals) is shown by the fact that they introduce it with equal consistency to disparate works, irrespective of whether the dialects of the originals had *-e* or not.

This evidence shows that the traditional argument is *not* circular. We are not inventing something on the basis of another unproven assumption (viz. that Chaucer wrote in decasyllables); we are doing no more than demonstrating that the assumption of a decasyllabic line agrees well with a grammatical distribution *known to have existed in south-eastern England in Chaucer's time and after*.

The same evidence enables us to estimate the status of Chaucer's language at the time he wrote. We know that from the mid fourteenth century onwards there were progressive types of London English in which *-e* no longer survived,[7] and that Chaucer must therefore have used what was, for the London of his time, a more formal, possibly more archaic, register, yet one which was well known and familiar because it partly coincided with the more conservative dialects of the neighbouring rural areas.

Secondly, more is now known than previously about the exact process of simplificatory changes like the loss of unstressed syllables. The view that such changes take place consistently and uniformly in all contexts is now outdated. Study of ongoing change[8] has shown that it takes place first in colloquial register, and is later transferred, though by no means evenly or consistently, to formal register. It is during this later stage that the newer and older forms may be selected from their different registers and combined, by a process of restructuring and differentiation, to form new contrasts (e.g. of stress) within the same register. It is wrong to say, therefore, that because the use or loss of *-e* is not 'consistent' throughout the written language of Chaucer, we must reject it as a metrical criterion. On the contrary, it is to be expected for that stage of the language that *-e* should perform a range of varied functions, some old, some new; in the adjective, its older uses survive almost intact, but in nouns and verbs it has undergone a restructuring to carry other distinctions. Thus for the verbs *had* and *were* we find that a syllabic scansion more often calls for monosyllables when they function as auxiliaries, but for disyllables when they function as lexical verbs.

Mr Robinson recognises that nouns with *-e* occur more often in formal use, those without in colloquial use. But he fails to recognise that the same formal contrast can expound different functions in different parts of the system, and that new distinctions of register or stress in nouns and verbs can combine with an older use in the adjective to form part of the total grammar of the text. In refusing to admit that such a combination of functions could exist, he is thereby led to the false conclusion that *-e* in the adjective is invalid as a metrical criterion.

One may suspect that the critics of the traditional view often do not appreciate the full significance of the linguistic details they discuss. Southworth's claim that *-e* had been lost everywhere long before Chaucer can be shown to be totally unfounded, and Mr Robinson is right not to follow him. But are his own attempts any nearer the mark? He proposes to replace the grammatical criterion for *-e* in the adjective by a rhetorical one. He has read through the occurrences of *hy(e)*, *heigh* 'high' in the Tatlock-Kennedy *Concordance*,[9] and quotes the following cases of a rhetorical, not grammatical, distinction:

(1) This goddesse on an hert ful hye seet
(2) Myn is the ruine of the hye halles
(3) To telle his hye roial magestee
His hye pride, his werkes venymus
(4) And short and quyk and ful of hy sentence
(5) Now looketh, is nat that an heigh folye

But, if the distribution of *-e* is rhetorical, it is by no means obvious that it is required in (1) or (2), whereas it is expected in (4) and (5). The distinction is grammatical, and if Mr Robinson cannot see that (1) demands an adverb, (2) and (3) a weak adjective but (4) and (5) a strong adjective, then there is no common ground for discussion.[10]

The traditional view of Chaucer's metre is the only one that fits the facts, and, since it is also that which does most credit to his skill, it presents no problem. But a problem which is only barely relevant to Chaucer arises when critics, intent on praising his followers above their worth, maintain that those lines of Lydgate, Hawes and others which are usually regarded as metrically deficient are in fact meritorious, and descend from what these critics claim to be the same practice in Chaucer.

In the case of Chaucer himself there is, as we have seen, no justification for this claim: it conflicts with the synchronic evidence both of Chaucer's text and other contemporary texts, and, since it is based only on later evidence, it is irrelevant. But in an attempt to provide a link with this later evidence, a specious chronological argument is advanced: that Lydgate lived so soon after Chaucer that he could not have lost an understanding of his metre, or, as Robinson puts it, forgotten his native tongue.

The answer to this has already been given above. It was not the *colloquial* speech of the previous generation that Lydgate 'forgot'. In the conservative register used by Chaucer, *-e* still had a specific distribution, but not in the colloquial register of his time; in the fifteenth century, *-e* survived as a possibility in speech, but in even more restricted use: it was reinforced less by conservatisms in other southern dialects, and, having lost its residual functions, was now no more than an optional ending in verse and perhaps other 'recited' registers. To equate this shift with 'Lydgate forgot his native tongue' just will not do. Chaucer's *-e*, though meaningful, was a conservative relic, the loss of which would not impair efficiency of communication; such a fall in the level of redundancy is always remedied, often by wholly different means such as increased periphrases elsewhere in the clause. Unless one of the forms happens to be of social significance as a prestige-marker, the speakers themselves remain unaware of such shifts.

There is nothing strange or unexpected about a specialised register which contains an archaic (or archaistic) *-e*. There are parallels in modern languages (e.g. French, German); even in modern English, we accept *-èd* as a poetic convention, and it is known that this applied also to *-e* as late as the sixteenth century.[11] The notorious 'broken-backed' lines can sometimes be explained as headless, or by a mid-line rest; but since an optional *-e* in verse is to be expected for this period, it is both unscholarly and perverse to deny it simply because it lowers our estimation of the verse. It is because they will go to any length rather than admit that Lydgate or Hawes used such expedients *metri gratia* that Southworth and Robinson insist that such poets used the device of giving a double syllabic measure to a single syllable. But the difficulty is that this device, if it is read into the text of these poets, appears merely pretentious and obtrusive, because it implies a degree of metrical sophistication which is not consonant with the poetic standard of their work as a whole. As used by a skilled metrist like

Hopkins, it undoubtedly succeeds; but it entails poetic heightening of a kind that the more pedestrian lines of Lydgate simply will not bear.

A possible exception to this is Wyatt. In his case, in spite of much talk about his use of natural spoken rhythms, there has been no close demonstration of the ways in which his original versions are superior to those of Tottel. If the differences are evaluated, they fall into two types: (1) lines in which Wyatt's 'freer' version does succeed in throwing emphasis on to thematic words, and (2) lines in which the freedom is merely otiose and akin to doggerel. The most we can say, therefore, is that Wyatt may, in a groping way,[12] have appreciated the resources of the device. But that is no reason for crediting Lydgate, Hawes, Barclay or even Skelton with such intentions, and in the case of Chaucer, there is strong evidence that we have no right to do so.

The fact that stress-timed metres continued throughout the period, especially in drama, is barely relevant to the issue. Naturally some discrimination is necessary when analysing the metres of a writer like Skelton, who combined both stressed and syllabic types; but this should not mislead us into accepting such combinations as a model in their own right. Robinson's 'balanced pentameter' is an attempt to reconcile Southworth's untenable view with the linguistic facts, but, even if his interpretations of the facts could be justified, the concept is neither sound in theory nor useful in practice. If we exclude from the argument all such 'verse' that is so free that it must depend on features other than metrical for its claim to the title, then verse must by definition be based on a metrical norm from which the poet deviates,[13] and this norm can be either stress-timed or syllable-timed, but not both. To propose that it should be both involves a contradiction which is not merely terminological, but robs us of our ability to give credit to the good poet for his effective variations. It is a commonplace that decasyllabic verse abounds in the speech-rhythms of Sievers's half-line types; but they contribute more to the variations than to the norm, and the two levels should not be confused. Again, obviously there are poets who oscillate between the two norms, and the passages where they do so can be judged on their merits. But to set up a norm that is so vague and all-embracing that it includes variations as 'normal' must defeat its own object.

Whatever one's opinions on Chaucer's English[14] followers, it is irresponsible to class Chaucer with them. Chaucer's chosen medium differed from theirs: its higher proportion of genuinely unstressed syllables gave it a delicacy and lilt similar to that of the earlier Middle English lyrics. The very simplicity of this medium is poetically satisfying, and it consequently requires fewer of the tensions and other variations that are the staple of later verse. A continual insistence on reading into Chaucer's poetry the merits we expect in later poetry is misjudged; it had its own merits, which have not been, and could not have been, achieved since his time.[15]

NOTES

1 I Robinson, *Chaucer's Prosody: a Study of the Middle English Verse Tradition*, CUP: Cambridge, 1971.

2 R T Davies, Review of Robinson, *Chaucer's Prosody*, *Review of English Studies*, new series 23, 1972, 190–2, p.191.

3 The fact that Chaucer uses elision more with some words than others (Robinson, *Chaucer's Prosody*, p.94) is of interest for anyone investigating Chaucer's linguistic sensibilities, but it is not relevant to the main point at issue.

4 See A McIntosh, 'A New Approach to Middle English Dialectology', *English Studies* 44, 1953, 1–11 (repr in *Middle English Dialectology*, chapter 2).

5 The list could be extended by at least ten other manuscripts known to the present writer, and further search would undoubtedly yield still more.

6 This manuscript of the *Southern Legendary* is by the same scribe as the Dulwich Coll MS of *Handlyng Synne* listed above.

7 This refers to Type II in the types of London dialect defined by M L Samuels, 'Some Applications of Middle English Dialectology', *English Studies* 44, 1963, 81–94 (repr in *Middle English Dialectology*, chapter 5).

8 See, for example, E Pulgram, 'French /ə/: Statics and Dynamics of Linguistic Subcodes', *Lingua* x, 1961, 305–25.

9 J S P Tatlock and A G Kennedy, *A Concordance to the Complete Works of Geoffrey Chaucer and to the Romaunt of the Rose*, The Carnegie Institution: Washington DC, 1927.

10 That this is in fact the case is suggested by Robinson's remark (*Chaucer's Prosody*, p.107): 'I don't know what to do with ''Stratford atte Bowe'' . . . But this is only to observe that even Homer nods; not all Chaucer's lines are good . . . ' Here, as in much of the rest of his argument, Mr Robinson does his poet no service; he is seemingly unaware that *atte* is an assimilated form of *at the*.

11 Cf. the references quoted by T F Mustanoja in his 'Chaucer's Prosody', in B Rowland ed., *Companion to Chaucer Studies*, OUP: Toronto, New York and London, revd edn, 1978, 65–94, p.67.

12 I have allowed the words 'in a groping way' to stand, but should emphasise that they are not intended as derogatory to Wyatt's merits as a poet; they refer rather to the low state of metrical theory and tradition at the time when Wyatt wrote.

13 The fact that completely 'normal' lines are rare is natural enough. The norm is still obvious because the variations occur in different places in the line, not always in the same place.

14 The Scottish 'Chaucerians' are not included here, since the dividing line between them and Chaucer is of a different kind. Final *-e* had been lost much earlier in the north, and Scottish poets had had a longer period in which to learn to handle the language in its changed state. Dunbar and Henryson may be 'Chaucerian' in certain other respects, but their linguistic medium differed radically from his in rhythm. In England, the corresponding skills were not fully attained till Marlowe and Shakespeare.

15 Since the first publication of the above, Professor Kirsti Kivimaa (Helsinki) has pointed out to me that there is a different way of proving quite conclusively that Chaucer wrote in decasyllables, viz. the fact that he availed himself extensively of pleonastic *that* after a high proportion of the available subordinators (e.g. *er*, *if*, *though*, *when*, *wher*, *which*, *whil*), and that he used this as a specific aid in fulfilling the requirements of his metre. To any fair-minded critic, this argument should suffice on its own; however, while the question of final *-e* remained under debate, there was always the possibility that it would be questioned. It is to be hoped that the combination of these two complementary arguments will now be accepted as conclusive. See K Kivimaa, 'The pleonastic *that* in relative and interrogative constructions in Chaucer's verse', *Commentationes Humanarum Litterarum* 39.3, Societas Scientiarum Fennica: Helsinki, 1966, and 'Clauses in Chaucer introduced by conjunctions with appended *that*', *Commentationes Humanarum Litterarum* 43.1, Societas Scientarum Fennica: Helsinki, 1968.

3 THE LANGUAGE OF GOWER

M L SAMUELS AND J J SMITH

The combination of linguistic features which characterises many of the earliest manuscripts of Gower's *Confessio Amantis* has long puzzled scholars. G C Macaulay, in his edition of the poet's English works, wrote that Gower's language 'is undoubtedly in the main the English of the court, and not a provincial dialect'.[1] Since Macaulay's time, however, our knowledge of the language of London in the fourteenth and fifteenth centuries has increased, and it has become questionable whether Gower's language can really be defined as the English of the court.

I

A pre-requisite for any new examination of Gower's language is that the most reliable text should be selected for analysis. Two English poems have been assigned definitely to the Gower canon: the *Confessio Amantis* and the short *In Praise of Peace*. There are many MSS of the *Confessio*, but the two earliest are MS Fairfax 3 in the Bodleian Library (F) and the 'Stafford' MS (S), once the property of the Earl of Ellesmere but now Huntington Library, California, EL 26 A 17. Macaulay used F as his base text. F was written by three scribes, a main copyist and two revising hands. S is in two hands, different from those in F: a main hand and one which supplied a missing leaf (fol. 50). For *In Praise of Peace*, Macaulay selected as his base MS the earliest copy of the poem, BL Addl 59495 (*olim* Trentham), which appears to be in the same hand as one of the revisers of F.[2]

F is an unusual MS in that it appears to have undergone three stages of revision:

(a) The original shape of the MS was that which Macaulay termed 'first recension'. At this stage which, for convenience, we might call F1, the MS had the original beginning and ending of the poem with the references to Richard II which were later excised.
(b) Then a second scribe added the later form of the ending over erasures and a replaced leaf. However, he appears to have retained the original prologue. Because of later activity, only book VIII, lines 2938–3146 remain from this stage (F2). This hand, perhaps, copied the Trentham MS.

(c) Finally, a third scribe carried out the revisions which produced the present text of this MS. We might term this stage F3. The scribe replaced lines 1–146 of the *Prologue* and lines 3147–end of book VIII. Latin additions of the same date put this stage after the fall of Richard II.

S, on the other hand, is what Macaulay termed a 'second recension' text. It always had the new prologue and epilogue found in the last stage of F (F3), but it also has disturbances in the fifth, sixth and seventh books, including some fairly lengthy extra passages.

S cannot have been the ancestor of F1 because F1 had the older beginning and end.[3] F1, therefore, must pre-date S. Since most of the text in F dates from the F1 stage, this can now be set aside, leaving us with the passages introduced and revised at F2 and F3. S is unlikely to have been the ancestor of the new passages in F2 because F2 only had the epilogue and it would have been logical in any copying of S by the scribe revising F to include the prologue—which S always had—as well. Although the passage remaining from this stage in F's revision is short, there are one or two errors in S which do not appear in F. However, these do not in themselves absolutely rule out the descent of F from S at this stage, as they are very small and could have been corrected by the scribe. It is more likely, although still only just possible, that S is the ancestor of the passages introduced at F3. The only place where F is correct and S is in error is at *Prologue* line 63 where F reads *To* against S *Tho*. Of course, this slight variation is well within the correcting capacity of a scribe.

We must now approach the problem from the opposite direction. F1 cannot be the sole ancestor (if ancestor it is) of S because of the additional passages in the fifth book which are not in F but are generally accepted as authorial.[4] F2 could be an ancestor for the epilogue but not the new prologue, because it did not have it. F is unlikely to have been the ancestor for S in its F3 form because of the late date (although this is not impossible).

The relationship between S and F in its various states can best, perhaps, be illustrated stemmatically:

Fig 1.

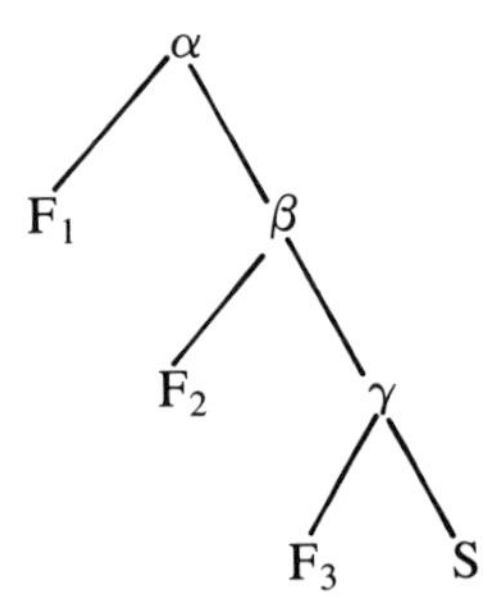

—where S = elements in S but not in F, and F1, F2 and F3 = elements introduced at F1, F2 and F3 respectively. α, β and, γ, of course, need not represent different MSS but, perhaps, simply an authorial copy undergoing continual revision. Unlikely, if just possible, stemmata which are alternatives to the above are:

Fig 2.

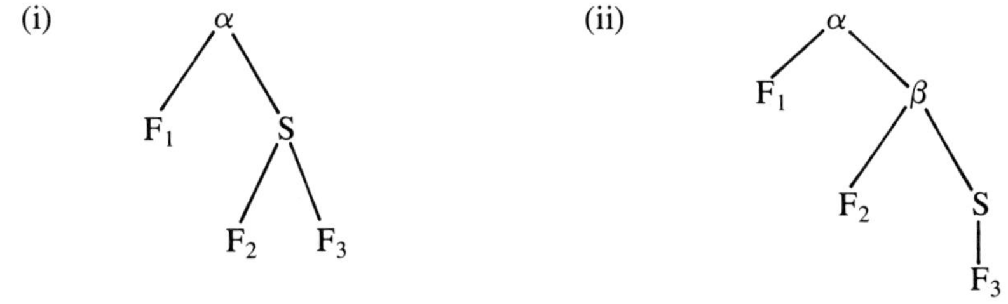

(These stemmata should not, of course, be taken as in any way a complete description of the relationship between the many MSS of the *Confessio Amantis*. They simply illustrate a local relationship.)

We can say, therefore, that there are passages in F and S which are definitely (rather than probably) independent. In F, these make up the main body of the text, leaving aside the lines introduced at F2 and F3. In S, the additional passages in books V and VII—which cannot be copied from F, which has never had them—are authorial, and must come from a line of descent independent from that of F as far back as the archetypal revision which produced the second recension.

Despite this independence of descent, the additional passages in S display exactly the same idiosyncratic linguistic features found in F. These features (some of which are discussed below) are also found in the Trentham MS of *In Praise of Peace* and, to a greater or lesser extent (although often less consistently) in most of the earlier MSS of the *Confessio*. It seemed, therefore, a reasonable working hypothesis (to put it no higher) that this language, found throughout the Fairfax and Stafford MSS, was the best choice for further analysis. We decided to adopt that course and to see where it led.

II

A predictable result of this analysis was that the language is not consistent with the dialect of a single area: whatever area was tried, there were always 'recalcitrant' forms that could not be accommodated.[5] The natural deduction was that it must contain forms from more than one dialect and, in attempting to pinpoint these dialects, we isolated two features that occur in separate and non-contiguous areas, both of them distinct from London:

(i) *oghne* 'own' (adj.). This occurs otherwise in pure Kentish texts only, and never in London texts except as a result of copying from a Kentish exemplar (see fig. 3, line A, and texts 1–6 on accompanying list).[6]

(ii) *or. . .or*, 'either. . .or'. This may occur sporadically from separate and independent developments of OE *oþer*, and is often influenced by Latin *aut. . .aut*; but the main area where it is most clearly part of the spoken language is limited to SW Suffolk and the adjoining parts of S Cambs. and NW Essex, as shown by line B on the map, and texts 7–13.[7]

It is a frequent practice of dialect researchers, when faced with two conflicting features of this kind, to attempt a geographical compromise, and to localise their text in some intermediate position such as mid-Essex or London. Such a conclusion could never be any more than pure surmise, and is here contradicted by the total absence of both forms from the texts of those areas. On the contrary, the occurrence of two such 'indexical' features suggested to us that the language might contain two distinct dialectal strata, each capable of fairly precise localisation. When we proceeded on that hypothesis, we found that there were indeed two sets of mutually exclusive features. In one set were features corroborating the Kentish stratum demanded by *oghne*:

(a) contracted 3rd person singular present indicative verbs, used to a far greater extent than in Chaucer, e.g. *makþ*, *falþ*, *arist*, *fint*, *wepþ*.
(b) *ie*-spellings as the reflex of OE ē, ēo and OF ē, e.g. *lief*, *diere*, *hiere* ('here' and 'hear'), *flietende*, *sieke*, *hiede*, *whiel*. The principal area for these spellings is W Essex and W Kent.
(c) *selver* 'silver': a Southern and SW Midlands form.[8]
(d) *soster* 'sister': primarily Kentish and South-Western.[9]
(e) *þerwhiles (þat)*, 'while': Kentish, with a narrow belt from there into the South Midlands, including earlier London texts.[10]

The other set included the following:

(a) *boþen* 'both': found in Norfolk, Suffolk and an area in the W Midlands.[11]
(b) *ȝoue* 'given': primarily an Eastern form.[12]
(c) *-h-* as in *myhte*, *hyhe*, *yhen*. For the principal Eastern manifestation of this, see lines C and D and texts 14–20.[13]

This second combination cannot be other than East Anglian and, when plotted on a map in combination with the diagnostic feature *or* 'either', showed that this stratum is to be localised in the triangle in SW Suffolk bounded by Bury St Edmunds, Clare and Lavenham.

Interesting support for these two strata came from certain minority variants in the Fairfax MS which Macaulay had normalised and recorded only in footnotes to his text:

(i) *schat* 'shalt' occurs in a belt running from central Norfolk down to W Suffolk and E Cambridgeshire. Since this form is very rare elsewhere, it would be surprising if it did not belong to the SW Suffolk stratum here.[14]
(ii) *wordle* 'world' is a typically Southern form which matches well with the Kentish evidence already quoted (it is the normal form in the *Ayenbite of Inwyt* and William of Shoreham).[15]
(ii) *wich* 'which' is not found in texts from E Kent, where the expected forms are *which* or the more archaic *hwich* and *huich*. But forms without *-h-* are found in texts from W Kent (e.g. *weche* in William of Shoreham) and this distinction therefore not only supported the evidence for a Kentish stratum but suggested W Kent as its provenance.[16]

After this assignment to two strata, the prominent feature *syh* 'saw' (pret.) remained, and this could not be accounted for in the Suffolk stratum. It was a form that was known in London (Chaucer rhymes on *sy* once, though usually on *say*) but it seems never to have been a regular London form in the fourteenth or fifteenth centuries.[17] We returned, therefore, to the Kentish part of the map, to find three instances: *sigh* (sg. and pl.) in MS Rawlinson Poet. 14, *isiȝe* (pl.) in William of Shoreham and *siȝe* (sg.) in Cambridge UL Ff III.11.[18] This feature, together with the occasional *u* as the reflex of OE *y*, as in *gulteles*, *gultif*, *hull* 'hill', tended to confirm NW Kent as the localisation of the Kentish stratum (see line E on map).[19]

The establishment of two dialectal strata in a text is, of course, a fairly commonplace procedure, and the more usual conclusion is that they originate from successive copyings by two different scribes, or, occasionally, that one stratum is that of the author and the other that of the copyist. In this case, however, there remained a crucial fact that militated against either of these conclusions: in each stratum, there is at least one feature that is proven by metre to be authorial. In the Suffolk stratum, there is *or. . .or* (instead of the more usual *oþer. . .or* and *either. . .or*) and perhaps also *boþen*; and in the Kentish stratum, the high proportion of contracted 3rd person singular present indicative forms, and *þerwhiles* (Chaucerian *whil*). To claim that the remaining (non-metrically attested) features are due to Gower's scribes would be perverse, for the following reason. The orthographical system attested by the Fairfax and Stafford MSS is very regular and consistent. If, in spite of this consistency, we insist that the non-metrically attested features are scribal and not authorial, we are forced to assume that the scribe or scribes possessed the same two strata in their language as those demanded by the metrically attested features. This, though just conceivable, is so extremely unlikely as to render the contrary virtually certain: that the combination of the two strata, including minutiae of spelling, is due to Gower alone, and that it reflects two separate regional influences in his upbringing, NW Kent and SW Suffolk. Furthermore it should be noted that, since the extra dialectalisms found in the Fairfax MS also belong to both strata, the same argument applies to them. Indeed, it may well be that the original authorial version contained many more such forms, which were partly eradicated by the Fairfax-scribe and wholly so by the Stafford-scribe.

III

In the normal way, a conclusion such as the above, based as it is on linguistic evidence alone, would doubtless be laid aside as unverifiable hypothesis, and there the matter would rest. In this case, however, there is important external evidence to confirm it. Gower's family owned land at Kentwell in SW Suffolk, precisely within the Bury St Edmunds—Clare— Lavenham triangle that we had already determined as the most likely source of one of the strata, and had associations with Otford in NW Kent.[20] Such a startling correspondence of linguistic and historical evidence enables us to assume with some confidence that Gower's formative years were spent partly in Kent and partly in Suffolk. Since

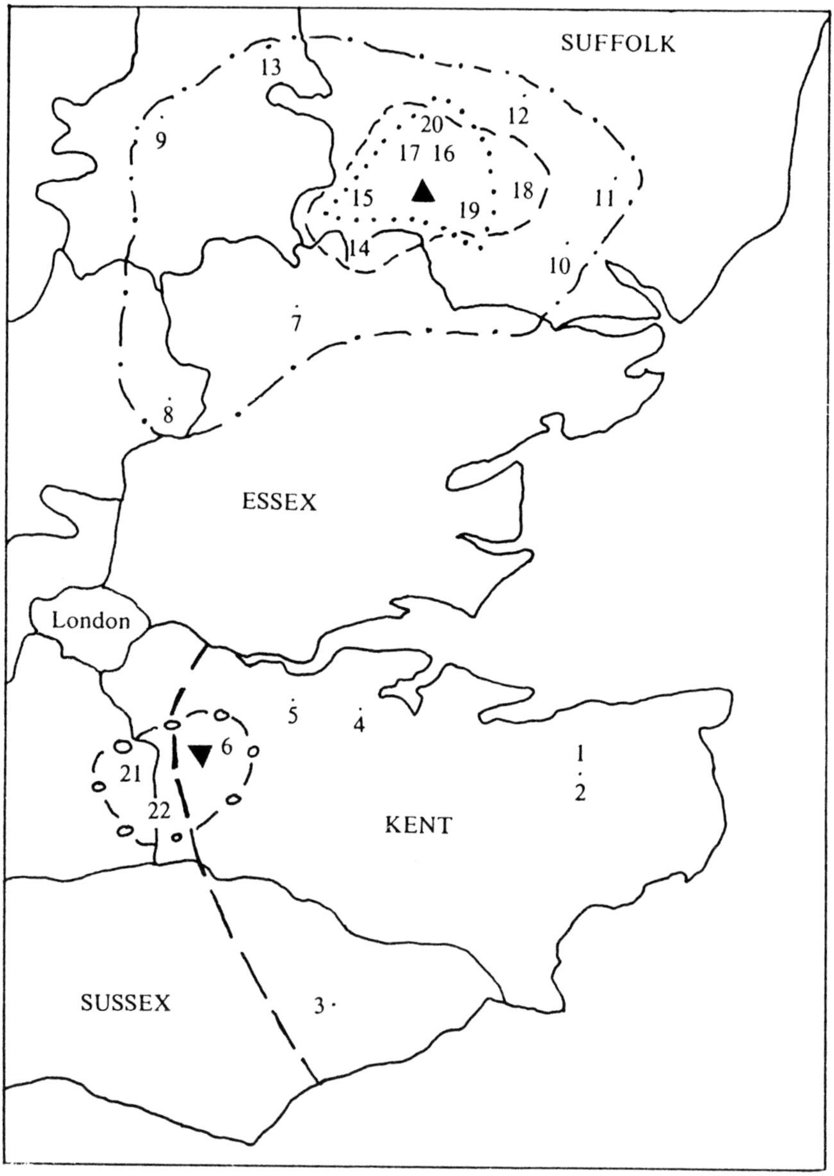

KEY A ———————————— *oȝene, oghne* 'own' Fig 3.

B -.-.-.-.-.-.-.-.-.-.-.-.-.-.-.-. *or . . . or* = 'either . . . or'.

C ------------------------------ *myhte*

D .... *hyh(e), hih(e)*

E °—°—°—°—°—°—° *sigh, sy* 'saw'

▲ Kentwell, Suffolk

▼ Otford, Kent

The numerals on the map denote texts, as follows:
1 BL Arundel 57 (Dan Michel, *Ayenbite of Inwyt*): *oȝe(ne)*.
2 CUL Addl 6845 (Ordinances of St Lawrence, Canterbury): *oghene*.
3 BL Sloane 3285, fols. 33–92 (Medica): *oghne, oughne, owghne*.
4 New Coll Oxford 92: *oȝene*.
5 Bodl Laud Misc 471 (Sermons): *oghe*.
6 BL Addl 17376 (William of Shoreham): *isiȝe, oȝe(ne)*.
7 BL Addl 37677: *or. . .or*.
8 Huntington Cal., HM 147 (*Book of Vices and Virtues*): *or. . .or*.
9 Bodl Tanner 17 (*Southern Legendary*): *or. . .or*.
10 BL Harley 211: *or. . .or*.
11 BL Harley 4011 (Bokenham, *Mappula Angliae*): *or. . .or*.
12 BL Sloane 340 (Medica): *or. . .or*.
13 St John's Oxford 138 (*Prick of Conscience*): *or. . .or*.
14 BL Arundel 327 (Bokenham, *Lives of Holy Women*): *myht*.
15 BL Egerton 2864 and Addl 5140 (*Canterbury Tales*): *hih(e), myht(e)*.
16 BL Harley 2278 (Lydgate): *hih, hyh, myhte*.
17 Durham University Library, Cosin V.iii.24: *myht*.
18 BL Egerton 3245 (*Prick of Conscience*): *myht(e)*.
19 BL Cotton Julius B.ii (*Chronicles of London*): *hyh, myht*.
20 Will of John Baret of Bury: *hih, hyh*.
21 Bodl Rawlinson poet. 14 (*Partonope of Blois*): *sigh*.
22 CUL Ff. III.11 (Prose *Merlin*): *sye*.

the Kentish stratum contributes so basic a grammatical feature as the contracted 3rd singular of verbs, it is presumably to be given priority; but that does not lessen the cogency of the view we now urge: that Gower's dialect is essentially based on the two regional dialects of Kent and Suffolk, not on that of London, as Macaulay thought. Naturally, Gower must later have been subject to some London influences; but, when we consider the rate at which the language of London was itself changing in the late fourteeenth century, it does not seem to have left any very obvious imprint on that of Gower. It is sometimes said that Gower used an older, more conservative form of London English; but that older form has a large number of typical identifying features, only a few of which (by the coincidence of their Kentish origin) appear in Gower.[21] Indeed, the general impression that Gower's language resembles that of contemporary London is due to a purely coincidental parallelism in the development of both: the language of London was in process of moving from a southern to a midland basis, while Gower's own idiolect, in its amalgam of Kentish (Southern) and Suffolk (Midland) had, in microcosm, made its own parallel move in the same direction.

As for London English in the late fourteenth century, Gower's differences from Chaucerian usage are well known, and may now be more readily explained:

(i) *The treatment of the reflexes of OE ȳ̆*
Chaucer uses *i, y* normally but *e* occasionally in rhyme. Gower's practice is the opposite—*e* more commonly in mid-line, but *i, y* in rhyme. This is understandable if he was combining Kentish and Suffolk usages, for in East Anglia *e*, though common, was restricted to fewer words belonging to the group than in Kent. We must assume that Gower was accustomed to both variants, and that *e* was his normal and preferred written variant, but that for rhyme he preferred *i* in order to conform with the commoner London usage.

(ii) *The present participle*

Gower's form, *-ende*, was a minor variant in Kent where the main form was *-ynde*, and in the mid-fourteenth-century London dialect where the main form was *-ande*. Chaucer, who must equally have grown up using some form in *-nde (-ande* or *-ende)*, adopted the more progressive *-ynge*, but Gower's persistence with *-ende* can be explained only by reference to the Suffolk stratum in his language; it was here that his original (Kentish) variant *-ende* received full reinforcement so that it became his normal form.[22]

IV

Our conclusion that Gower wrote, and presumably spoke, in a mixture of two identifiable regional dialects cannot, of course, be treated in isolation. From a literary viewpoint, one may speculate on whether this mixture might have lowered him in the estimation of his contemporary audience. The probable answer is that it would not have constituted any disadvantage to him in his lifetime, since no standardised form of the written language then existed; it was only after 1430 that such differences could have been measured by the yardstick of the emergent written standard, and even by that time it would not have spread sufficiently for the differences between it and Gower's forms to attract (or distract) the attention of the average early-fifteenth-century reader. By the late fifteenth century, naturally, such differences from the standard would be noticed, but by that time they would be regarded as differences of period rather than of dialect.

Secondly, from a more purely linguistic viewpoint, Gower's language can now be regarded as a case-history for fourteenth-century sociolinguistic development. Hitherto, study of the origins of standard English has been virtually restricted to the growth of a written standard. It has seemed reasonable to assume that there was a parallel growth of a spoken standard which, if not accorded actual priority over the written standard, must surely have interacted with it in its growth; yet the evidence for it is naturally scanty,[23] and it has remained largely a matter of surmise. The combinations of features found in Gower's language are obviously not due to poetic artifice of the Spenserian type; but they can, on the contrary, provide evidence of that process of adaptation in speech habits which, especially if it occurred on a large scale among those who migrated directly to London, could well account for the growth of a spoken standard at this early period. However, the case of Gower is suggestive of more than this. A successful spoken standard requires a wide regional basis, which is supplied not only by actual immigration to the capital, but also by a continuing approximation of different surrounding dialects caused by speakers who combine them as the result of travel or migration. Viewed in this way, the very fact that scholars have for so long regarded Gower's language as close to that of the court is significant, for it adds a further dimension to our knowledge of the process leading to the formation of a spoken standard.

These and doubtless other aspects of this subject must be reserved for further discussion. For the present, however, its most obvious and immediate relevance is for the text of Gower. It is now not too much to claim that the Fairfax and

Stafford MSS are, in all respects except their actual handwriting, as good as autograph copies, and that the text of Gower's work has been authenticated to an extent far greater than is likely to be possible for the copied works of any other author at such a remove in time.

NOTES

1 G C Macaulay ed., *The English Works of John Gower*, Early English Text Society extra series 81–2: Oxford, 1900, Vol I, p.cxx.

2 For further details of the text as it appears in MSS F and S, see Macaulay, *English Works*, pp.cxxvii ff..

3 This point is emphasised because recent studies on the textual transmission of copies of Gower's *Confessio Amantis* have revealed the complexity of the problem. See A I Doyle and M B Parkes, 'The production of copies of the *Canterbury Tales* and *Confessio Amantis* in the early fifteenth century', in M B Parkes and A G Watson eds, *Mediaeval Scribes, Manuscripts and Libraries: Essays presented to N R Ker*, Scolar Press: London, 1978, 163–210. A new collation of the Gower MSS is now in progress under the direction of Professor Derek Pearsall. Until this is completed, any statement as to the relationships between MSS of the *Confessio* must remain provisional.

4 There are also some short passages in F1 but not in S. Unfortunately, they are too short to yield significant linguistic information. Since they could have been introduced or excised in copying, they are not to be taken as evidence of the priority of S or F, even though they appear to be authorial.

5 For the method used in localisation, here and elsewhere in this article, see A McIntosh, 'A New Approach to Middle English Dialectology', *English Studies* 44, 1963, 1–11 (now repr in *Middle English Dialectology*, chapter 2), M Benskin, 'Local archives and Middle English dialects', *Journal of the Society of Archivists* 5, 1977, 500–14, and *LALME*, Vol I, 1–36 (subsequent references to *LALME* in this chapter are to maps).

6 Cf. *LALME* I.499, II.202.

7 *LALME* I.405.

8 *LALME* I.1065.

9 *LALME* I.517.

10 *LALME* I.255.

11 *LALME* I.369.

12 *LALME* I.432.

13 Cf. *LALME* I.333, II.53, 149.

14 *LALME* I.1190.

15 *LALME* I.292.

16 *LALME* II.11.

17 The only writer to use it commonly is Hoccleve, and it is of interest to note that his use of it would fit, and indeed support, the suggestion that his birthplace was Hockcliffe, Beds. But irrespective of whether that suggestion is accepted, his spelling in many ways shows imitation of Chaucer, so that it would not be surprising if for this feature he had imitated Gower.

18 *LALME* I.514, II.211.

19 Cf. *buylde* in Caxton (Mn *build*), which is presumably due to Caxton's origins in W Kent.

20 See entry in the *Dictionary of National Biography* for John Gower; also J H Fisher, *John Gower: Moral Philosopher and Friend of Chaucer*, Methuen: London, 1965.

21 See M L Samuels, *Linguistic Evolution*, CUP: Cambridge, 1972, p.167. Of the eighteen features listed there, only three appear in Gower: *dede* 'DID', *þerwhiles* 'WHILE', and *-ende* present part. (where *-ande* is the commoner London form).

22 *LALME* I.348–9, II.57.

23 See E J Dobson, 'Early Modern Standard English', *Transactions of the Philological Society* 1955, 25–54.

4 CHAUCER'S SPELLING

M L Samuels

The problem of how Chaucer spelt is a long-standing one, on which new opinions have been expressed in the past decade.[1] But there are now also new sources of evidence which have not yet been considered. Firstly A I Doyle and M B Parkes have shown conclusively that the work of the two scribes who copied four of our earliest manuscripts of the *Canterbury Tales* was not limited to Chaucer, but that it also included manuscripts of Gower.[2] Secondly, the spelling of the Fairfax and Stafford MSS of the *Confessio Amantis* has been authenticated as that of Gower's in a quite unexpected way,[3] and that provides us with an essential control for examining the copying habits of the two scribes already referred to. Thirdly, more is now known about the history of the language of London in the fourteenth and fifteenth centuries than was available to earlier scholars like Koch[4] and Wild,[5] and there is thus a fuller frame of reference for the evaluation of the new evidence.

I

It will be convenient to explain the frame of reference first. In my article 'Some Applications of Middle English Dialectology' (1963)[6] the main London type to ca.1380 was designated Type II, while 'Chaucerian' English of ca.1380–1420 was called Type III. It is not intended here to revise that typology, which was based on certain striking differences, especially *þat i(l)che* 'the same', *werld, warld* 'world', and *eld(e)* 'old' in Type II compared with *þat ilke, thilke, world,* and *old(e)* in Type III. Nevertheless, the texts belonging to these two types were admitted to show considerable variation on other criteria. If we now place those texts in an order that is roughly chronological, and trace the fluctuations and more gradual changes shown by the other criteria, it should then be possible, by a refinement of the typology, to show what combination of features might be expected at given points in the fourteenth and early fifteenth centuries. The texts to be considered, in their more detailed classification, are as follows.

A. *Early and mid fourteenth century, Type* II

1 Auchinleck MS (Edinburgh, Advocates 19.2.1), main hand.

2 Auchinleck MS, hand 3.[7]
3 The Early English Prose Psalter in BL Addl 17376.[8]
4 St John's, Cambridge 256.

B. *Late fourteenth century, Type* II
5 Magdalene, Cambridge Pepys 2498, Bodl Laud Misc 622, and BL Harley 874, all in a single hand.[9]

C. *Late fourteenth century, Type* III
6 The documents of East London provenance in R W Chambers and M Daunt, *London English 1385–1425*, pp. 47–57, viz. Gilds of St Katherine's, Aldersgate, Sts Fabian and Sebastian, Aldersgate, and St Paul's (Pouchmakers). These are selected as especially relevant to Chaucer's place of upbringing in Upper Thames Street.
7 Petition of the Folk of Mercerye, ibid., pp.33–7. This is included because, of the remaining fourteenth-century London documents, it is that which is closest to those given in 6 above, and can therefore usefully add to the range of forms available for comparison.
8 Peterhouse, Cambridge 75.I of the *Equatorie of the Planetis* (hereinafter *Equatorie*).[10] On the claim that this is in Chaucer's own hand, F N Robinson (Preface to his second edition of Chaucer's works) commented: 'Later investigation, while by no means disproving, has not conclusively substantiated this claim.' The reasons for including it here will appear later.

D. *Early fifteenth century, Type* III
9 The Hengwrt and Ellesmere MSS of the *Canterbury Tales*, i.e. NL Wales, Peniarth 392 and Huntington, Cal., 26.C.9 respectively.
10 Corpus Christi, Cambridge 61 of *Troilus and Criseyde*.
11 Trinity, Cambridge B.15.17 of *Piers Plowman*.
12 Huntington, Cal., HM 111 (*olim* Phillipps 8151) and 744 (*olim* Ashburnham 133), and other autograph MSS of Hoccleve.[11]

E. *ca.1430 onwards, Type* IV (*'Chancery Standard'*)[12]
13 Typical forms in documents written by Chancery-trained scribes, in PRO, Early Chancery Proceedings and Exchequer TR Council and Privy Seal.

The result of applying eleven variational criteria to the above thirteen texts (or groups of texts) is shown in the table on pp.28–9, and this will be used as the frame of reference for the discussion that follows.

II

Of the new sources of evidence already mentioned, the most important is the scribe of the Hengwrt and Ellesmere MSS, who has now been shown to have been the second of the five scribes who copied from Book II, l. 2686 to the end of Gower's *Confessio Amantis* in Trinity, Cambridge R.3.2 ('Scribe B' in the nomenclature of Doyle and Parkes).[13] As a copyist of Gower, this scribe is very unusual in that he translates his Gower exemplar thoroughly (with a few notable exceptions) into the normal Hengwrt-Ellesmere spelling. That he was copying from a conventional Gower exemplar can be shown, firstly, by the relict forms from Gower in the other hands of the manuscript, and secondly by this scribe's habit of using *-ee-* for Gower's typical *-ie-* even in words where, when copying Chaucer, he would not have used *-ee-* at all, e.g. *mortal* in Hengwrt-Ellesmere but *morteel* and even *mortiel* (3.2027) in Gower. A similar pointer is his use of *thei* as well as *they* when copying Gower, but of *they* only when copying Chaucer. These features agree with the now authenticated text of Gower,[14] but for most other features the gap between the two spelling-systems is very wide, as may be seen from the following comparison of regular forms from the Fairfax MS of Gower and Scribe B's stint in the Trinity MS:

Fairfax	Trinity	Fairfax	Trinity
þese	thise	mochel	muchel
tuo	two	yit,yet	yet
sche	she	togedre	togidre
ȝoue	yeue	hyhe	highe
her(e) 'their'	hir(e)	ferst	first
eny	any	euel	yuel
-ende	-ynge	oghne	owene

This imposition of an entirely different spelling-system on the Gower text is in itself interesting because it suggests (though it could hardly be held to prove) that the spelling so familiar to us from the Hengwrt and Ellesmere MSS is really that of Scribe B, not that of Chaucer. There may, of course, have been a closer similarity between Scribe B's and Chaucer's spelling than between Scribe B's and Gower's, and one could even posit the extreme view that Scribe B had learnt, or developed, his spelling system from continually copying Chaucer. However, Middle English scribes fall into various categories according to the consistency with which they copy literally or translate into their own spelling, and Scribe B clearly belongs to the latter category. He transforms Gower's spellings with such obviously practised ease and consistency that it is difficult to believe that he was acting any differently when he copied Chaucer.

If Scribe B's spelling is primarily his own, what can he tell us about Chaucer's? The answer is that for just a few items he shows forms that are 'constrained' by those of his exemplar. This practice was common in scribes who in other respects were thorough translators, and must be distinguished from the mere copying of forms alien to the scribe's normal practice. To use the terminology of the most recent discussion of the subject,[15] Scribe B was here activating certain forms from his 'passive repertoire' under the influence of his exemplars. By comparing his treatment of certain items when copying from different exemplars, we can deduce which forms he would normally write and which derive from his exemplar (see table at top of page 26).

Naturally, it is not always possible to be certain of the scribe's own

Fairfax MS of Gower	SCRIBE B Trinity MS (Gower)	SCRIBE B Hengwrt-Ellesmere MSS (Chaucer)
aȝein	ayein	*agayn(s), *ageyn(s), ayeyn(s)
tofore((afore))	tofore((afore))	biforn, bifore
worche, werche	werche	werke, *wirke
sih,	saugh,	saugh,
syh,	seigh,	seigh,
sawh	*sigh(e)	*say, *saw

preferences, but one can at least be sure that certain forms were *not* those that he normally wrote, and these are marked with an asterisk. The forms for 'before' are evenly balanced; his use tells us which were in his exemplars, but not whether he had a preference or used them all in free variation. On the other hand, his normal form for Gower's *sih, syh* is *saugh*; *sigh(e)* is obviously a constrained usage, while *seigh* is most probably his own rarer variant which he used under the influence of his exemplars' forms, whether *sih* (Gower) or *say* (Chaucer).

From the above it may be fairly deduced that the following were in B's Chaucer exemplar: *agayn(s)*, *ageyn(s)*; *biforn*, *bifore*; *wirke*; *say*, *saw*. Furthermore, since editors and textual critics are fairly generally agreed that the Hengwrt and Ellesmere MSS are close to the archetype of the *Canterbury Tales*,[16] it is reasonable to postulate (if only provisionally at this stage of the argument) that these forms are archetypal.

Another scribe who contributed to the Trinity MS of Gower is relevant here: the fourth hand, accordingly called 'Scribe D' by Doyle and Parkes. Their discoveries here are even more dramatic, for they show that this scribe also copied MSS Harley 7334 and Corpus Christi, Oxford 198 of the *Canterbury Tales*, and, in addition, no fewer than nine other manuscripts, including seven of the *Confessio Amantis*. For our present purposes, however, this scribe is less promising, for three reasons. Firstly, his exemplars for the *Canterbury Tales* were less close to the archetype than those of the Hengwrt and Ellesmere MSS; secondly, his own dialect was probably not that of London;[17] and thirdly, his copying habits are less straightforward and predictable than those of Scribe B. His active repertoire admits of more variants, including, apparently, some that he has adopted from his work of copying, and the result is that some obviously 'Gowerian' spellings appear even when he copies Chaucer.[18] Nevertheless, amidst all this mixture, it is still possible to detect some differentiation in his forms for 'not' and 'such':

copying Trevisa[19]	copying Gower	copying Chaucer
nought, nouȝt, not, noȝt, nouȝ	nought, nouȝt, not, noȝt, noght, nough	nought, nouȝt, not, *nat
such(e), soche, *swiche	such(e)	such(e), *swich(e)

Since Scribe D's exemplars for the *Canterbury Tales* had passed through one or more Northern and Midland stages of copying, it is all the more remarkable that the Southern form *nat* survived, and this provides strong evidence that *nat* is the archetypal Chaucerian form; and the same may reasonably be assumed (though again only provisionally at this stage of the argument) regarding *swich(e)*.

In addition to the above new evidence, an older source—that of rhymes—may be considered here. It is often regarded with suspicion, since one can always claim that a form was used purely to achieve the rhyme, and that it was not the poet's normal form. Indeed, that will hold true of the forms for 'not', for although, as we have seen, there is evidence to support *nat*, *noght* was obviously more convenient for rhyming purposes and is Chaucer's normal rhyme-word for the negative. However, that objection does not apply to the variants for 'yet'. The rhyming indices[20] show that Chaucer rhymed commonly with words ending in both *-et* and *-it*, and that he had available to him a wide range of words with both endings; but he invariably rhymed on *yit*, not *yet*. Since there is evidence for both variants in London in the fourteenth, fifteenth and sixteenth centuries,[21] there seem no valid grounds for rejecting the rhyming evidence that Chaucer's form was *yit*.

To sum up so far: the evidence points, with varying degrees of cogency, to the following eight forms as authorial or, at least, archetypal: *swich(e)*, *agayn(s)/ageyn(s)*, *yit*, *biforn/bifore*, *nat*, *wirke* (vb.) 'work', *say* and *saw* (past tense) 'saw'.

III

If we now return to the table on pp.28–9, it is remarkable how closely the above list of forms tallies with those in column 8 (the *Equatorie*) in practically every detail,[22] and that it tallies with those of that column *and no other*. Even if we grant that some of the indications gathered from our new evidence are hypothetical rather than factual, the resulting correspondence of the two sets can hardly be due to pure coincidence, and our attention is immediately drawn to the four forms *moche(l)*, *shollen*, *yif*, and *thorw*, in which the *Equatorie* differs from the traditionally 'Chaucerian' *muche(l)*, *shulle(n)*, *if*, and *thurgh* of Hengwrt-Ellesmere. Here, the most striking and relevant fact is that all four (but especially *yif* and *thorw*) are such as might be expected for Chaucer both chronologically and dialectally:

(i) *moche(l)* was a well-established London variant, as may be seen from columns 2, 4, 6, 7, 12, and especially 6 (East London documents contemporary with Chaucer); furthermore, Scribe B wrote *muchel* for Gower's *mochel* (which suggests that *muchel* was B's own form), and his occasional *moche* when copying the *Canterbury Tales* is therefore quite probably influenced by his exemplar.

(ii) *shollen* is paralleled as a variant in columns 2 (*sscholle*), 6 (*schole*), and 7 (*sholle*); the *o*-forms seem to have been ousted by *u*-forms c. 1400, in the same way as *sholde* was to be ousted by *shulde* some two to three decades later.

	1 Auchinleck, main hand	2 Auchinleck, hand 3	3 Early English Prose Psalter	4 St John's College MS	5 Pepys, Laud, and Harley MSS	6 East London documents
SUCH	swiche	swich(e)	swich swyche	swich(e) suich	swich suich	swich(e)
MUCH	miche(l)	moche(l) ((muche))	michel mechel	mochel(l) muche(l) miche(l)	mychel	moche
SHALL pl.	schul(len)	sschulle sscholle	shul(le) schul	schulle(n) (schul(n))	schullen	schul(le) (schole)
IF	ʒif ((if,ʒiue))	ʒif	ʒif,ʒyf ((if))	ʒif((if))	ʒif	ʒif
AGAIN(ST)	oʒain(s) oʒe(i)n oʒaines	aʒen ((aʒein))	oʒain(s) oʒayn(s) (oʒaines aʒeins aʒayn)	aʒein(s) aʒain(s) aʒayn agein	aʒein(s)	aʒen(s)
YET	ʒete	ʒit (ʒet)	ʒete ʒit	ʒit ʒete	ʒutt ((ʒut))	— —
BEFORE	bifor(e) biforn (tofor(n))	bifore biforn (tofore toforn)	tofor(n)e (aforn)	tofore(n)	tofor(n)e bifor(n)e	byfore byforn beforn before (afore)
NOT	nouʒt no	nowt	nouʒt (noʒt, nauʒt)	nouʒt (noʒt nauʒt	nouʒth (no)	nat (nouʒt nauʒt)
WORK vb.	wirche (werche, wirke)	—	wirchen wyrchen	werke werchen	wirchen	werche
THROUGH	þurth	þourgh (þour(g) þourgʒ þourh)	þurʒ þourʒ (þurwe þurʒt þur(t)h)	þorw (þourw þoruʒ)	þorouʒ (þorou)	thorwʒ thurwʒ (thorw þurwʒ)
SAW pret.	seyʒe seiʒe (seye)	segh(ʒ) seʒ segʒ(e)	seiʒ(e) (saiʒ)	se(y)ʒ sei	seiʒ	—

USE THIS!!

7 Petition, Folk of Mercerye	8 Equatorie	9 Hengwrt- Ellesmere	10 CCCC 61	11 Trinity Coll. Cambridge B.15.17	12 Hoccleve	13 Chancery Standard
such(e)	swich(e)	swich(e) ((such(e)))	swich (such)	swich(e)	swich	such
moch(e)	moche(l)	muche(l) (moche, meche)	muche(l) (michel)	muche(l)	moche, -il	muche (moche)
shulle sholle	shollen	shulle(n)	shullen	shul	shul(n)	shul(l) shullen
if(yif)	yif	if	if	if	if	if
ayein(s)	agayn(s) (agains)	agayn(s) ageyn(s) ayeyn(s)	aȝein(s) aȝeyns agayn(s)	ayein(s)	ageyn(s) agayn	ageyns(t) ageyn(e) (ayein(st))
yet	yit	yet	ȝet	yet	yit	yit yet
bifore(e) (afore)	byforn (byfore)	biforn bifore	biforn byfore	before tofore (afore)	toforn beforn before	before afore
nought	nat	nat noght	nought nouȝt nat nauȝt	noȝt	nat (not)	not
—	wirke wyrk workest	werken wirkyng	werken	werche	wirke	werk(e)
thourgh	thorw	thurgh	thorugh ((thorwgh))	þoruȝ	thurgh	thorugh
—	say	saugh (seigh say saw(e))	saugh (sey seigh say saigh sauȝ)	seiȝ sauȝ	sy	sawe

(iii) *yif* is of especial interest since, although this text is predominantly Type III, it is distinguished chronologically by this form from the fifteenth-century Type III texts. For this feature, the *Equatorie* is classed with the older Type II and with the East London documents of Chaucer's time.

(iv) *thorw* 'through' is less in evidence in texts of Type II, which usually show *þourgh*, *þurȝ*, *þurth* or similar forms; but it does appear in column 4, with a variant *þurwe* in column 3. Since the main forms throughout the fourteenth century were variants of *þurȝ* (reappearing as *thurgh* in Scribe B), it is possible that *thorw* was a local East London variant; it is surely significant that *thorw* and the related forms *thorwȝ* and *thurwȝ* appear in column 6, in the very documents that come closest of all in localisation to Chaucer's place of upbringing. In any event, further support for the form as one appropriate to Chaucer comes from *wherthorw* in the Appeal of Thomas Usk.[23]

Thus the combined evidence resulting from the application of all eleven criteria provides very strong support indeed for the view that the *Equatorie* is in Chaucer's own spelling. If the combination is viewed historically as a late-fourteenth-century London system, only one feature of it arouses comment, and that is the use of *-g-*, not *-y-*, in *agayn(s)*. Such forms are not typical of Types II or III; *aȝen(s)*, *aȝein(s)*, *ayein(s)* are normal in the late-fourteenth-century documents, including the Appeal of Thomas Usk and the Proclamations of Nicholas Brembre[24] (which are not represented in the table on pp.28–9). *Ayeyn(s)*, *ayein* seem likewise to have been Scribe B's preferred forms (cf. p.26 above), and the same is quantitatively true of the scribe of Corpus Christi Cambridge 61: probably both these scribes used *agayn(s)* only when influenced by their exemplars. Lastly, *ayein(s)* is the form used in another early-fifteenth-century Type III text (column 11). It is thus difficult to escape the conclusion that *agayn(s)* was an exceptionally progressive form for Chaucer to use. Since it was to form part of the written Chancery Standard in the fifteenth century, it was doubtless well enough known as a spoken form in late-fourteenth-century London. We may surmise that Chaucer's adoption of it was due to his having encountered it more than most Londoners as a man of travel and affairs, but, since so pronounced a feature is more likely to have been adopted earlier in his life, it might equally well be due to his period of service as a page at Hatfield, Yorks., in the later 1350s. But whatever the reason for this form, the very fact that it is unexpected yet vouched for by both Scribe B and the *Equatorie* is in itself significant.

IV

If the view urged above is accepted (viz. that the *Equatorie* is our best evidence of Chaucer's spelling), a number of further questions immediately arise. How does it relate to Chaucerian textual criticism and editorial policy? Are these features, singly or in combination, to be found in any subsequent manuscripts of Chaucer's work? If not, what is the explanation? Why is a prominent feature like *thorw* not represented in those manuscripts usually regarded as nearest to their archetype (Hengwrt, Ellesmere, Corpus Christi, Cambridge 61)?

These questions are by no means easy to answer, but three general points may be stated in advance:

(i) The number of forms replaced is not large. Many remained in fifteenth-century Type III texts, so that typical features that we have grown accustomed to call 'Chaucerian' are in fact common to both the *Equatorie* and Hengwrt-Ellesmere: *thise* 'these', *hir*(*e*) 'their' as well as 'her', *swich*(*e*), *sholde*, *byforn*/*byfore*, *nat*.

(ii) In a period of increasing standardisation (at least regionally and locally, if not yet universally), it was inevitable that a certain proportion of variants should disappear.

(iii) If the variants do reappear in fifteenth-century manuscripts, we have to assure ourselves, by examining the other linguistic features of those manuscripts, that they are not the result of translation into dialects in which such variants still naturally occurred.

Of the variants in question, *thorw* is the most outstanding and in need of explanation. Accordingly, in what follows, 'through' may conveniently be adopted as a test-word.

Perhaps the best example of the problems that are encountered is CUL Gg.4.27 (*Canterbury Tales*, *Troilus*). This manuscript is generally agreed to be high in the stemma of the *Canterbury Tales*, and some have even regarded it as equal in authority to Hengwrt-Ellesmere.[25] Its main forms for 'through' are *þorw*, *thorw*, *þour*, *thour*, with less common *þorow*, *thorugh*, *tho*(*u*)*rgh* and *thurgh*. Since the dialect is a very pronounced East Anglian one into which *thorw* and *thour* fit exactly, it is reasonable to assume that these are the scribe's own forms, and that *thorugh*, *tho*(*u*)*rgh*, and *thurgh* come from exemplars. However, since this manuscript has been suggested as a better representative of Chaucer's spelling than Hengwrt-Ellesmere,[26] we need better proof that this allocation of forms is correct. The proof comes from another manuscript written by the same scribe, Bodl e Musaeo 116 (Mandeville and *Astrolabe*), where the only forms are *thorw*, *thour*, *thourw*. Since both manuscripts are written fairly consistently in the same dialect, it is difficult to see why the scribe should add *thorugh*, *tho*(*u*)*rgh*, *thurgh* in Gg. unless those were the exemplar's forms; and the presence of *thurgh* suggests that this manuscript goes back to a copy in the same later Type III language as Hengwrt-Ellesmere (that there was at least one intermediate stage of copying is shown by western relict forms). Other features for which Gg. has been praised as authentic (like the endings in *-ys*, *-yth*) are, like *thorw*, mere concomitants of its East Anglian dialect.[27]

The great majority of the rest of the *Canterbury Tales* MSS show *thurgh*, *thorugh*, and *through* or variants of these forms (*þurgh*, *þurȝ*, *þorgh*(*t*), *thorgh*, *thurh*, *þourh*, *thoruh*, *thorowȝ*, *thoro*(*u*)*gh*, *thorou*, *thorow*, *thorouȝe*, *throuȝ*, *throuh*, *throwe*, *thrugh*). It is relevant to note that even of these MSS the proportion of dialectal MSS is high, and can be explained only by assuming that many London MSS of the early fifteenth century were written by immigrant scribes.

Only a very few contain *thorw* or related forms *þorwhe*, *thorghw*, and, here again, it belongs to their uppermost layer of dialect, as in the Lansdowne MS (SW Midlands) and the Delamere MS (NW Kent).[28] Although it is always possible that a more exhaustive search might prove the contrary, the strong impression remains that there are no manuscripts of the *Canterbury Tales* that can be proved to go back to a stage of the language earlier than the late Type III of Hengwrt-Ellesmere. We can only assume that *thorw* was replaced by *thurgh* at some point high in the stemma, or that it was replaced more gradually by successive copyings. If the evidence of the earliest MSS of the *Canterbury Tales* is considered to be more relevant than that of the rest, then the former explanation seems more probable.

If such a simple explanation is available in the case of the *Canterbury Tales*, the problem of the *Troilus* MSS is more complex. A longer period of copying and lost manuscripts antedates our first surviving ones of the early fifteenth century. Even the possibility of an antecedent copy in a language closer to Type II is not to be entirely ruled out, for Corpus Christi, Cambridge 61 contains a thin sprinkling of such forms: *ich* 'each',[29] *noither* 'neither',[30] *ar* 'ere', *therwhile* 'while',[31] *werld* 'world',[32] *sygge* 'say'.[33] But Corpus Christi, Cambridge 61 is predominantly 'late Type III', and its claim to represent Chaucer's language is poorer than that of Hengwrt-Ellesmere, for its normal form for 'through' is *thorugh*, and this is unlikely to be original as the metre always presupposes a monosyllable, not a disyllable. (At II. 616 there is the single, tantalising instance of *thorwgh*.)

A *Troilus* MS which might at first sight seem more attractive as a link with the *Equatorie* is St John's, Cambridge L.I, since it contains the form *thorw* together with *yit*, *yit*, *swich*, *shol* pl. 'shall', *sholde*, *biforn*, *nat*, *thise*, *hir*(*e*) 'their' and 'her', *any*, occasional *ageyn*, and *say* 'saw'. But this apparent agreement is illusory, for there are in fact three layers in this text—a 'Chaucerian' layer, a northern layer, and a third (uppermost) layer in the language of a scribe from the borders of SE Shropshire, NE Herefords and NW Worcs. This last is shown by striking features like *-nn-* in words like *gronne* 'groan', *cheynne* 'chain', *-uu-* as in *thouusand*, and the forms *thikke* 'the same' and *-lische*, *-lysche* for the adverbial ending '-ly'. The forms *thorw*(*e*), *thor*(*w*)*gh, thorght* exactly fit the localisation of that W Midland layer,[34] and the same probably applies to *yit*, *yif*, *shol*, and *sholde*. Once again, therefore, the Chaucerian layer is reduced to no more than the usual sprinkling of late Type III forms.

In BL Harley 2280, the position is similar. There are again three layers: Type III, shown in *thise*, *swich*, *nat*; Northern, shown by *scho*, *walde*, *omange*, *ath* 'oath', *sla* 'slay', *twa*, *gud*; and SW Midland, shown by *swuche*, *mony*, *fram*, *worldeles* gen. sg. 'world's'. Here, just as in the previous case, it is far more likely that *þorwgh*, *þorwh*, *þorwȝ* belong to the SW Midland layer and not to the Chaucerian one. In other MSS of *Troilus* (e.g. the Campsall MS and Harley 1239), *thorugh*, *thorow* (whether Type IV or dialectal) is the commoner form, but *thurgh* also occurs occasionally, suggesting that such MSS may also have passed through the normal 'late Type III' stage of copying.[35]

Thus, in the case of the *Troilus* MSS, the evidence does not even suggest a simple solution; it does not, this time, indicate that there might have been a stage, high in the stemma, at which *thorw* was replaced by *thurgh* or *thorugh*. That may, of course, have happened, but the evidence suggests no more than that it was gradually replaced by repeated stages of copying. Occasionally it may have survived because it happened to coincide with the dialectal copyist's regular form, but this cannot be proved; and there is no MS of *Troilus* in London language that preserves *thorw*, unless we are to consider the stray *thorwgh* in Corpus Christi, Cambridge 61.

As was pointed out earlier, if viewed historically, the disappearance of *thorw* from both of the main Chaucerian MS traditions is not surprising. Though it is well supported by the relevant documents as the form that Chaucer might have used, it was never more than a minority variant in London and, especially if it was subject to repeated copying, was bound to be ousted by the better established Type III form *thurgh* and by the increasingly common *thorugh*, a variant in Type III and the normal form in Type IV.

V

It might be objected at this point that if there are no manuscripts of authentic works of Chaucer that preserve genuine and specific traces of the type of spelling used in the *Equatorie*, then, in spite of the chronological and dialectal evidence in its favour, the case for it remains unproven. But that would be unjustified, for not only does the type recur, but it recurs in manuscripts of two independent prose works of Chaucer, *Boece* and the *Astrolabe*.

CUL Dd.3.53[36] of the *Astrolabe* is clearly in two layers of language, one of which tallies with that of the *Equatorie* and the other belonging to a copyist. The copyist's forms do not amount to much more than a veneer, for he leaves many unchanged: *she*, *hir*, *swich*, *shal*, *wole*, *fro/from*, *than(ne)*, *yif*, *yit*, *agayn(s)*, *byforn*, *nat*, *seyn/sein* (inf.). Others he occasionally alters, leaving two strata, as follows:

exemplar	copyist	exemplar	copyist
thise	the(e)s, theise	whan	wan
it	hit	after	aftur
which(e)	wiche, wych	wirke, wyrke	werken
euerich	euerech	thorw	thorow, thorgh
any	eny, ony	-ed, -id	-et
moche(l)	mechel, michel	first(e)	furst(e)

CUL Ii.3.21 of *Boece* is a more complex case since its uppermost layer is in the language of the NW Kent-London border; and because the dialect of the scribe was quite close to that of his exemplar, the layers cannot be differentiated for every item. Obvious Kenticisms of the scribe are the *-y* infinitive ending (*answery*, *gadery*, etc), *brengeth* 'brings', *by* 'be', *on-* 'un-', *seuende* 'seventh'; but other forms tally with those of the *Equatorie*: *thise*, *swiche*, *any*, *yif*, *yit*, *byforn*, *nat*, *myhte*, *thorw*. Those that occur in doublets will fit the two layers, as shown in the table below. In only one case did the copyist wholly reject his exemplar's form: he wrote *ayein*(*s*) and *ayen*(*is*), not *agayn*(*s*). But this is not at all surprising, for the same tendency existed in many other copyists of Chaucer (cf. p. 30 above).

exemplar	copyist	exemplar	copyist
it	hit, hyt	thilke	thikke, thykke
whiche	weche, wych	world	wordyl
moche(l)	meche	fro, from	fram
shol(len)	shellen	lasse	lesse
wolt	welt	whan	wan

The fact that the type of language found in consistently written form in the *Equatorie*, without scribal variants, recurs with an extra scribal layer in MSS of two known works of Chaucer can hardly be accidental. It adds strong support to the view advanced above regarding Chaucer's spelling, and, although it is not the purpose of the present article to urge more than that, it increases the likelihood that the *Equatorie* is an authentic and autograph work of Chaucer.

VI

Of the questions posed above on p.30, one still remains—that of editorial policy. The *Equatorie* is a short text which could not provide a model complete enough for the wide-ranging lexis of Chaucer's major works. The *Boece* and the *Astrolabe* are longer, but they contain layers of language, and since only the more obvious boundaries between their layers can be ascertained, they too are not suitable as models. It might be possible to establish some kind of consensus from all three texts, but that is a task that lies in the future. Failing that, probably the nearest an editor could get at present to Chaucer's spelling would be to take a consensus of Hengwrt-Ellesmere and Corpus Christi, Cambridge 61 and then, wherever feasible, to alter spellings in the directions indicated by the *Equatorie*. But that is not a counsel that would appeal to all editors; for those who prefer a single text, Hengwrt-Ellesmere is probably somewhat nearer to the truth than Corpus Christi, Cambridge 61; but which of those two, Hengwrt or Ellesmere, is to be preferred? The differences between these two MSS pose a problem, for although in general the forms used overall are the same, their distribution in the two MSS varies considerably, the earlier type of variant being more frequent in Hengwrt, the later type in Ellesmere. Examples are: *-o-* vs. *-ou-* in words likc *ynogh*, *thogh*, *thoghte*; *-a-* vs. *-au-* in words like *draghte*, *faght*; *seigh*, *say*, vs. *saugh*; *neigh*, *heighe* vs. *ny*, *hye*. Furthermore, Hengwrt shows more cases of the noun plural in *-is*, which also occurs in the *Equatorie* and is supported by rhymes. It is difficult to tell whether these differences are due to changes in preference over a fairly long period in the scribe's life, or merely to the constraints of differing exemplars. If the former were the case, the order of copying must necessarily be Hengwrt-Ellesmere; if the latter, then either order of copying is possible. This problem, too, requires further study, but for our present purpose a solution is perhaps unnecessary: Hengwrt preserves a higher proportion of early spellings, and, if that is one of the editor's criteria, he can choose accordingly.

The conclusions reached above may be summarised as follows. New evidence available from the study of scribal habits in the earliest surviving manuscripts of the *Canterbury Tales* suggests that the only manuscript to preserve Chaucer's spelling is that of the *Equatorie of the Planetis*, and this evidence is supported by rhymes and by chronological and dialectal evidence. The same spelling system survives in contaminated form in two later MSS, one of *Boece*, the other of the *Astrolabe*. Many of the identifying features of this spelling coincided with that of the local London standard of the early fifteenth century, and are therefore represented in the best MSS of the *Canterbury Tales* and *Troilus* (Hengwrt, Ellesmere, Corpus Christi, Cambridge 61). But certain remaining features, notably *thorw* and *yit*, found no place in this local standard, and were therefore replaced in the normal process of copying. Since it is not practicable for editors to extrapolate on a large scale from the *Equatorie*, they have the choice of adopting the spellings of Hengwrt as they stand, or of modifying them in the direction of those of the *Equatorie*.[37]

NOTES

1 M B Parkes and R Beadle, Introduction to *Poetical Works of Geoffrey Chaucer: A Facsimile of Cambridge University Library MS Gg.4.27*, Brewer: Cambridge, p.47, n.40 and reference there quoted.

2 A I Doyle and M B Parkes, 'The production of copies of the *Canterbury Tales* and the *Confessio Amantis* in the early fifteenth century', in M B Parkes and A G Watson eds, *Mediaeval Scribes, Manuscripts and Libraries: Essays presented to N R Ker*, Scolar Press: London, 1978, 163–210.

3 M L Samuels and J J Smith, 'The language of Gower', *Neuphilologische Mitteilungen* 82, 1981, 295–304 (repr as chapter 3 above).

4 J Koch, *A detailed comparison of the eight manuscripts of Chaucer's Canterbury Tales*, Chaucer Society: London, 1913.

5 F Wild, *Die sprachlichen Eigentümlichkeiten der wichtigeren Chaucer-Handschriften*, Wiener Beiträge zur englischen Philologie 44: Vienna, 1915.

6 M L Samuels, 'Some applications of Middle English dialectology', *English Studies* 44, 1963, 81–94 (now repr in *Middle English Dialectology*, chapter 5).

7 The principal works in this hand are *The Seven Sages*, *Floris and Blauncheflur*, *Sir Degare*, and *The Assumption of the Virgin*.

8 K D Bülbring ed., *The Earliest English Prose Psalter*, Early English Text Society original series 97: London, 1891.

9 For published portions, see M Goates ed., *The Pepysian Gospel Harmony*, Early English Text Society original series 157: Oxford, 1919; G V Smithers ed., *Kyng Alisaunder*, Early English Text Society original series 227: Oxford, 1947; J Påhlsson ed., *The Recluse*, Universitets Årsskrift: Lund, 1911.

10 D J Price ed., *The Equatorie of the Planetis*, CUP: Cambridge, 1955.

11 See Doyle and Parkes, 'The production of copies', p.182, and, for texts, F J Furnivall ed., *Hoccleve's Minor Poems I*, Early English Text Society extra series 61: London, 1892, and I Gollancz ed., *Hoccleve's Minor Poems II*, Early English Text Society extra series 73: London, 1897.

12 For the term 'Chancery Standard' see Samuels, 'Some applications' (now repr in *Middle English Dialectology*, chapter 5).

13 Doyle and Parkes, 'The production of copies', p.170. Recently, in *Studies in Bibliography* 35, 1982, 133–54, R V Ramsey has attempted to show that the Hengwrt and Ellesmere MSS are by different scribes. I answer his case in 'The Scribe of the Hengwrt and Ellesmere Manuscripts of the *Canterbury Tales*', *Studies in the Age of Chaucer* 5, 1983, 49–65 (repr as chapter 5 below; cf. also chapter 6 below.)

14 Samuels and Smith, 'The language of Gower'.

15 M Benskin and M Laing, 'Translations and *Mischsprachen* in Middle English Manuscripts', in M Benskin and M L Samuels eds, *So meny people longages and tonges: philological essays in Scots and mediaeval English presented to Angus McIntosh*, MEDP: Edinburgh, 1981, 55–106; now largely reproduced in *LALME*, Vol I, General Introduction 2, 2.2–2.4; 3, 2–5; and appendices.

16 See, e.g., F N Robinson ed., *The Works of Geoffrey Chaucer*, OUP: Oxford, 2nd edn, 1957, p.xxxvii.

17 He has a greater tendency to use western forms than other London scribes. It follows that his use of *þ* and *ȝ* is not of chronological significance.

18 For scribe D's work as a copyist, see chapters 6 and 9 below.

19 In MS BL Addl 27944. To judge from the other two hands, this MS was copied in London from an exemplar in language containing dialect strata from both London and elsewhere.

20 W W Skeat, *Rime-Index to Chaucer's Troilus and Criseyde*, Chaucer Society: London, 1892; Isabel Marshall and Lela Porter, *Rime-Index to Chaucer's Minor Poems*, Chaucer Society: London, 1889; H Cromie, *Ryme-Index to the Ellesmere Manuscript of Chaucer's Canterbury Tales*, Chaucer Society: London, 1875.

21 For the sixteenth century see E J Dobson, *English Pronunciation 1500–1700*, OUP: Oxford, 2nd edn, 1968, Vol II, para. 77.

22 The past tense 'saw' occurs only once, as *say*. The absence of *saw* is therefore not significant, especially since *say*, as the earlier form, is the more important.

23 R W Chambers and M Daunt eds, *A Book of London English 1384–1425*, OUP: Oxford, 1931, pp.22–31.

24 Chambers and Daunt, *Book of London English*, pp.31–3.

25 See n. 1 above.

26 See n. 1 above.

27 It is true that there are some similarities between late-fourteenth-century East London texts and those of East Anglia, and these may perhaps have been caused by immigration. But that is no reason for selecting an East Anglian MS of Chaucer's works and pronouncing its language to be authentic.

28 Admittedly a *dialectal* connection between the Delamere MS and the *Equatorie* can be traced, for its *thorghw* (*thorwe*) belongs to the same enclave as the *thorw* of the *Equatorie*. But its language is of such a late and idiosyncratic kind that it could not be

considered as even a remotely connected descendant of a manuscript written in the same language as the *Equatorie*.

29 *Troilus and Criseyde* III.1690, V.831.

30 *Troilus and Criseyde* III.938.

31 *Troilus and Criseyde* III.538.

32 *Troilus and Criseyde* IV.1580.

33 *Troilus and Criseyde* IV.194.

34 As evidence for this layer, two W Midland MSS may be compared: Bodl Addl B.107 (*Castle of Love*), and Trinity, Oxford 16A (*Prick of Conscience*).

35 Many of the *Troilus* MSS are specifically dialectal and need not be considered here. Examples are MSS BL Harley 3943 and 4912, Bodl Selden B.24, Selden Supra 56 and Digby 181.

36 The resemblance of the language of this MS to that of the *Equatorie* was noted by R M Wilson in his section on the language in Price's edition, pp.146 f.

37 In 'The Scribe of the Hengwrt and Ellesmere Manuscripts' (reprinted as chapter 5 below), I have now shown that the Hengwrt MS must be regarded as having been written earlier in the career of the scribe than the Ellesmere MS, and that the first of the alternatives given on p.35 above is the correct one.

5 THE SCRIBE OF THE HENGWRT AND ELLESMERE MANUSCRIPTS OF *THE CANTERBURY TALES*

M L SAMUELS

I

The singular number of the word 'scribe' in the title is intentional. Recently R Vance Ramsey[1] has questioned the view of A I Doyle and M B Parkes[2] that on palaeographical grounds these two manuscripts are the work of a single scribe and insists that they are by separate scribes. He admits that the hands are 'identical' and states that they are so because his two scribes received identical training. He quotes no parallels for such a phenomenon, and it is doubtful whether he could do so for any but Chancery-trained scribes. Suffice it here to say that he is not arguing with the palaeographers; he has conceded them their case and has chosen to argue his own purely from spelling practices. So be it. He has chosen his position, but it is a difficult one, for it places the onus on him to prove that these texts could not have been written by one man, while taking full account of, first, what is known about the spelling practices of scribes in the later Middle English period and, second, what is known and to be expected by way of variation or standardisation in the London language of a particular period, 1390 to 1420.

Ramsey inherits from Manly and Rickert the notion that the early manuscripts of *The Canterbury Tales* are 'standardised'[3] and assumes from that that the rest of their language, apart from the points of difference that form his case, can be taken for granted. But this procedure is unjustifiable, for much more is now known about the language of London in this period than was available to Manly and Rickert. As I have shown elsewhere, there was no standardisation in London to the degree that he postulates until the emergence, ca.1430, of what I have termed Chancery Standard, or Type IV.[4] Before that time there are three other types that may be considered, but of these only Type I (Central Midland Standard) comes anywhere near the kind of homogeneity postulated by Ramsey, and obviously our scribe does not partake of it, whereas Types II and III are terms of convenience that embrace a series of heterogeneous London texts in the period 1340 to 1420, including our scribe as one of the evidently separate and individual contributors to Type III.[5] During this whole period, apart from Type I, the spelling of each scribe is idiosyncratic, and can be distinguished as such from every other by application of a special questionnaire of at least one hundred common variables in spelling that was devised for the Middle English Dialect Survey at the Universities of Edinburgh and Glasgow.[6] The result, for the whole survey, is some 3,500 linguistic 'profiles' of separate scribes.[7] When the questionnaire was applied to the Hengwrt and Ellesmere manuscripts, they were found to agree for all variables except a few in which there was a difference of emphasis in the proportion of variants found in each manuscript, e.g., *agayn/ayeyn*, *aske/axe*, *heighe/hye*, *hundred/hondred*, *murye/myrie*, *neigh/ny*, *noght/nought/nat*, *seigh/saw/saugh*, *thogh/though*, *thowsand/thousand*, *weere(n)/were(n)*. Since none of these forms was exclusive to one manuscript, the profiles for both manuscripts were regarded as those of a single scribe who had slightly changed his habits and/or had come under the influence of varying exemplars.

Now when Ramsey states that the usages of individual Middle English scribes could not alter in this way, he is simply ignoring a great deal of evidence to the contrary. There is, first, the detailed study by M Benskin and Margaret Laing,[8] showing that it was normal for scribes to possess repertoires of spellings, variants from which became activated under different circumstances of copying. Then, especially for the fifteenth century, Norman Davis has shown how Edmond Paston gradually changed his original Norfolk spellings in the direction of standard English, even to the extent of proceeding by intermediate stages, e.g., first from *xal* to *schal* and finally to *shall*.[9] Furthermore, writers who changed their habits in this way were not rarities: there is a large body of similar evidence for other writers in the fifteenth century.[10]

Especially relevant to the period when Hg and El were produced is Doyle's recent study of University Coll, Oxford 97.[11] He shows the shifts of scribal habit that took place in the three separate sections written by the single scribe of folios 85–185 and, after careful consideration of all the possible factors involved, concludes that the changes are 'intelligible as adaptation to the fashions of a metropolitan milieu about 1400' and that 'a contrary hypothesis is not easily tenable.'

The principle of changes in scribal habits is thus a well-established one, and Ramsey's denial of it cannot be justified. Such changes could, however, be brought about by two different kinds of pressure, and, since in what follows both will be found to apply, they must first be distinguished.

II

A frequent cause of variations in spelling in the work of a single scribe is the influence of his exemplar. For Ramsey this matter is cut and dried: either the scribe takes over the form of the exemplar exactly, or he uses his own, single and monolithically fixed, form. But the matter is by no means as simple as that. For some items a scribe's usage *always* admitted of variants. For example, a Norwich scribe might normally use *swych*, *sweche*, and *swylk* in free or conditioned variation (his 'active' repertoire), but be quite prepared to use other forms he was familiar with like *such* or *sich* (his 'passive' repertoire).[12] It can be proved from manuscripts in which the same scribe copied several works from different exemplars that he would select the variant that was nearer that of his exemplar (though not necessarily the identical form), and the same applies to different manuscripts in the hand of a single scribe. As an example I choose here two manuscripts not used by Benskin and Laing in their article: BL Addl 34779 of *Piers Plowman* (C version) and Manchester Rylands English 90 of *The Prick of Conscience*, both so outstanding in their common idiosyncrasy of script, duct, and spelling as to leave no doubt that they are in the same hand. In the Rylands manuscript there are several extra variants conditioned by the Northern exemplar; e.g., the scribe writes here *mekel* as well as his normal *meche*, *ilk* as well as his normal *uche/vche*; but otherwise the spelling is reasonably consistent throughout both manuscripts. There are, however, two notable exceptions:

1 For 'are' the scribe uses three forms, *ben*, *arn*, and *ar*, throughout both works but with opposite proportions in each: in *Piers Plowman*, *ben* is predominant; in *The Prick of Conscience*, *ar*(*n*). In other words, the forms are the scribe's own, but the proportions of them are influenced by those of the exemplars, though these were not necessarily the same forms.
2 For 'through' he writes exclusively *þruȝ* in *Piers Plowman*, but *þurgh* and *þurȝ* (and variants) in *The Prick of Conscience*, with only a very rare *þruȝ*. There is thus no indication of the scribe's own preference; all we know is that he had both forms in his repertoire and could use either, consistently and for long stretches of text, according to circumstances.

The conclusion to be drawn from this, and from many other similar examples,[13] is that, under the influence of an exemplar, certain of a scribe's own forms can vary in their proportions or even undergo a virtually 100 percent shift, while the remainder of his usage remains constant throughout.

The second kind of pressure toward change in spelling belongs especially to the later Middle English period (i.e., the late fourteenth century onwards) and amounts simply to this: if changes in practice are taking place, or if there is oscillation from competing practices, scribes observe this in their exemplars and shift some of their own practices accordingly. As pointed out above, in London ca.1400 there was as yet no specific standard for scribes to aim at, but there were pressures on them to alter their habits nevertheless. The spelling practices current in London had only recently undergone a complete metamorphosis in the change from Type II to Type III;[14] in addition, the period from 1400–20 was crucial for the development of Standard English, for it was from the competing and changing fashions in spelling at this time that the new written standard was to evolve. Some typical changes in train at this time are the replacement of *þ* and *ȝ* by *th*, *y* and *gh*, of *e* and *o* by *ee* and *oo* when denoting long vowels, of *þeigh* by *þough* and *though*, and of *say/seigh*, 'saw', by *saw* and *saugh*. As I have attempted to show elsewhere,[15] these changes were due largely to immigration from the Central Midlands, and it was midlanders who were setting the pace in the changing spelling of the capital. Besides these, there were two other tiers of scribes who would start from different thresholds of spellings and therefore achieve different repertoires, depending on how far they adapted to change: the native Londoners, and immigrants from parts other than the Central Midlands, notably the North, the NW Midlands, and the SW Midlands. The immigrant scribes might react in two ways: they might continue to use their regional spellings in London, thus contributing to the confusion by wholly exotic forms, or they might attempt to adapt their own regional spelling systems to what they conceived to be more acceptable in London, thus contributing more subtly to the confusion. That there were northerners of the former type at work in London ca. 1400 is shown by some curious relict northern strata in certain manuscripts in which such contaminations are the last thing that would be expected (e.g., BL Harley 7334 of *The Canterbury Tales*, the Lansdowne manuscript of the same, and BL Addl 27944 of Trevisa's *De proprietatibus rerum*); while the continuing use of *þ* and *ȝ* is especially noticeable in the work of scribes who had migrated from the SW Midlands (the Petworth manuscript of *The Canterbury Tales* and the upper stratum of the Lansdowne manuscript are examples of this).

There is, therefore, much evidence from manuscripts copied in London in the early decades of the fifteenth century of a variety of conflicting spellings, local and regional.[16] That there still existed scribes who wrote consistently and conservatively is not, of course, to be denied, but it cannot be too strongly emphasised that the preconditions for changes in scribal habits existed in full force. In particular, the lack of a common currency of spellings at which immigrant scribes might aim leads to some extraordinary shifts and vacillations. An outstanding example is the scribe who wrote BL Harley 7334 and Corpus Christi, Oxford 198 of *The Canterbury Tales*, as well as nine other manuscripts (including seven of Gower's *Confessio Amantis*).[17] Basically this scribe was attempting to adapt his regional SW Midland orthography to London use; however, when copying Chaucer, Trevisa and *Piers Plowman*, he would for some stretches use Gowerian forms that he had learned and added to his repertoire from copying Gower, whereas for other stints within the same manuscripts he returned, quite unpredictably, to his earlier repertoires of SW Midland and London forms.[18]

III

As has been shown above, there are scribes who show great versatility in learning new forms in mid career. Even if it is conceded that these are the exception rather than the rule, enough has also been said to show that a mere shift in the proportion of variants used within a scribal repertoire is not only commonplace but, especially at this period, to be expected in all but the most doggedly conservative of scribes.[19] And what else is our Hengwrt-Ellesmere scribe but a straightforward example of such a shift? Of all the variables quoted by Ramsey, none is exclusive to one text; there is merely a shift in emphasis, not a change of repertoire. The scribe has not had to *learn* a new form. Ramsey quotes two so-called exceptions, but one is of a form that the scribe gives up (Hg *down/doun*, El *doun* only), and that leaves only *elles* as his one new form that partly replaces *ellis*; but both these cases are merely parts of the larger shift of *ow* to *ou* and *-is* to *-es*; they are extensions of existing habits to further contexts, not genuine innovations (a fact that Ramsey concedes when he combines all the different sequences with *ow/ou* into a single list). If these manuscripts were by separate scribes, we should expect at least a few substantive differences of spelling exclusive to each manuscript; but there are none.

Next: Is the size of the shifts as great as Ramsey makes out? He presents a superficially impressive table of so-called dominant contrasts between the two manuscripts, ranging from 60 to 99 percent. Now, although I showed above that there are proved cases of 100 percent shift in scribal habit, that was for the purposes of the argument only. In fact, Ramsey's method of counting and presentation has inflated the figures for each shift, in some cases to the extent of doubling or even trebling them. As he points out, his count is restricted to those cases where the two manuscripts differ and wholly omits the many cases where they agree.[20]

Let us take his column 7 (*þ^t/that*) as an example. For this he shows a 'dominant contrast' of 81.95 percent, from which the average reader might justifiably assume that $þ^t$ is the predominant form in Hg, *that* in El. Such an assumption would be entirely mistaken, however, as can be shown quite simply by counting *all* the cases of $þ^t$/*that* in a representative stretch of the texts. For this purpose I chose *The General Prologue* and the *Knight's*, *Miller's*, *Reeve's* and *Cook's Tales*, which must be admitted as a fair sample because, according to Ramsey's method of calculation, it would yield a 'dominant contrast' of 88 percent, not the 82 percent of his overall figure. In this stretch the total number of instances for comparison is 688, which shows that Ramsey, in restricting himself to 199 of them, has ignored 71 percent of the usage. The distribution of the 688 instances is as follows:

	Hg	El
$þ^t$	334 (49%)	181(26%)
that	354 (51%)	507 (74%)

The resulting shift is thus in reality no more than 23 percent, not 88 percent. Then, even if one were to discount all cases of line-initial *That* (and it is by no means certain that that would be methodologically preferable), the shift is still only 32 percent, not 88 percent. Admittedly, $þ^t$/*that* may be a rather extreme case of the discrepancy between Ramsey's figures and reality, but anyone considering his arguments would do well to bear in mind what his table of figures really represents: not a series of radical contrasts that must prove separate scribes but merely a series of shifts that is perfectly compatible with the work of a single scribe.

So much, then, for Ramsey's 'balance of probability'. He ignores a whole dimension of the subject: a large body of evidence for changes in scribal habits and, in particular, the special reasons for such changes in the period 1390–1420; and he compounds this omission by presenting figures that misleadingly exaggerate the differences in question. Of the total orthography of this scribe, only a minor part is affected, and then only by shifts of existing variants, not change of form; the rest remains the same idiosyncratic set of forms. Obviously, if one compares the same work in two copies word for word, the differences will be highlighted; but that is to lose sight of the way they agree when compared with the great bulk of other surviving Middle English texts. Add to this the identity of handwriting, and the balance of probability is clearly against Ramsey's view. There remains, however, a second whole dimension that he has ignored. When that is examined, it will be seen that this case is, in reality, very different, and no longer a mere matter of balancing probabilities.

IV

There is a peculiar mystery about Ramsey's article: Why, when he professes to challenge the view of Doyle and Parkes (and has presumably read their article), does he ignore the third text that they show to be also in the same hand, namely hand B of Trinity, Cambridge, R.3.2? I cannot credit that he has deliberately shut his eyes to it, and I can therefore only surmise that he has tacitly dismissed it as irrelevant, perhaps because he sees further spelling differences in it that would lead him to claim that it is by yet a third scribe, writing, again, in an identical hand (he could hardly deny the identity since he has already conceded it for the other two manuscripts). If this is so, he is evidently unaware that, when due account is taken of the constraints of the Gower exemplar, the linguistic profile for this text is identical with the profiles for Hg and El referred to in section I above. It so happens that we are now in a strong position to judge this, for the Fairfax and Stafford manuscripts of Gower's *Confessio Amantis* have been authenticated to an extent never hitherto thought possible for any mediaeval text other than autograph: they have been proved to be in language and spelling that is an entirely idiosyncratic mixture of two quite separate dialects, which in turn can be isolated and pinpointed exactly as those of two places in Kent and Suffolk that were associated with the Gower family.[21] That our scribe's Gower exemplar was in the same language can be proved from relicts in his version,[22] but it is his own treatment of the Gower text that stands out; for, whereas most of the early manuscripts of Gower attempt to reproduce the idiosyncrasies of their exemplars, this scribe has imposed on the Gower text the normal spelling familiar to us from Hg and El, and his concessions to Gowerian spelling are wholly transparent and therefore easily discounted. Thus, in addition to his normally consistent *they*, he also writes *thei* (or even *þei*) under the influence of Gower's *þei*; he consistently writes *ayein* (Gower *aȝein*), though that is his rarer variant elsewhere; and he is faithful throughout to Gower's *tofore*, which he must have regarded as quite distinct from Chaucer's *bifore/biforn*.

Since it can be shown that our scribe is influenced by his Gower exemplar, the next question that arises is: Could the differences between Hg and El stem from differences in his exemplars for those manuscripts? That explanation is not the main one proposed here, but it must be pointed out that Ramsey has too easily dismissed it as a possibility. His main objection, that the features in question should show an uneven distribution when the stemma affiliations change, will not bear examination, for one could postulate any number of intermediate exemplars, all of which preserved the same stemma confusions, but which—at least in the copy antecedent to El—had had all their inconsistencies in spelling homogenised by the translation process so frequent in Middle English. That explanation cannot, therefore, be ruled out, at least as a secondary source of variation; but obviously the more important hypothesis, and the one to which all our indications point, is that Hg and El represent stages of a progression in the career of our single scribe, the differences being due to changes in habit brought about by the second type of pressure defined in section II above. Here the evidence of the Trinity Gower is crucial, for, if the hypothesis is correct, this manuscript should fall into place as part of the progression. To test this, it is necessary to do what Ramsey has declined or omitted to do: to apply his differential criteria to hand B of the Trinity manuscript.

The result is everything that we might hope for from this accession of extra evidence: *the Trinity manuscript stands somewhat more than midway in a progression from Hg to El.* At the time when the Trinity manuscript was written, six of the shifts in emphasis had already taken place, three were in progress, and three had yet to come, as follows:

1 The shifts in proportion from & to *and*, *y* to *i*, *ay* to *ey*, single to double vowel, *-er-* to abbreviated *-er-*, and *-ow-* to *-ou-* had taken place.
2 The shifts from *h* to crossed *h*, *þ*[t] to *that*, and *d* to tailed *d* were in progress.
3 The shifts from *-on* to *-oun*, *-ogh* to *-ough*, and *with* to *w*[t] had not yet taken place.

There remain two points (the addition of final *-e* or *-n*) on which a statistical comparison with the Trinity manuscript is not practicable because of the differing metrical practices of Chaucer and Gower; but in any event, as will be shown in section VI below, these two features do not form part of the progression proper and are more probably due to a different cause. Of the points listed above, two call for further comment:

1 The distribution of *-ow-* and *-ou-* is the same as in El, with *doun* and *toun* as the regular forms but *thow* still occurring as a minority variant to *thou*.
2 The distribution of *þ*[t] and *that* is of especial interest. It changes twice, so that the text of Trinity must be considered in three sections (section 1, 3.793 to 3.1916; section 2, 3.1917 to 3.2708; section 3, 3.2709 to 4.2142). In section 1 the proportions are similar to those of Hg, with perhaps a suggestion that the shift has begun (41/59 percent compared with 49/51 percent in Hg). In section 2 the scribe succumbs to the influence of his exemplar and, reverting to what was certainly an earlier habit of his of using *þ* in words other than *þ*[t], takes over the Gowerian *þat* in addition to increasing his proportion of *þ*[t]; but in section 3, the proportion of *that* greatly increases, almost reaching the level seen in El. The intrusion of *þat* in section 2 (26 percent) complicates the issue, but it drops to 14 percent in section 3, and, since all cases of it are due to the exemplar and do not form part of the scribe's normal usage, it is reasonable to draw up a table of percentages of the majority *þ*[t]/*that* usage only (the percentage figures for Hg and El are included for comparison):

	Hg	Trinity Section 1	Trinity Section 2 (influenced by exemplar)	Trinity Section 3	El
þ^t	49	41	48	29	26
that	51	59	52	71	74

These percentages are obviously significant, but their exact interpretation requires care, depending as it does on the following three factors: (1) that the choice of *þ^t* would save space and/or labour, (2) that the distributions could be inherited from, or influenced by, those present in the exemplar, and (3) that *þ* was obsolescent in London by this period and being replaced by *th*.

At first sight the fact that *that* is favoured in El, the more lavish production, might seem to favour (1), but that is counterbalanced by exactly the opposite shift from *with* in Hg to abbreviated *w^t* in El. Although, therefore, the scribe may well have shifted his preference from *with* to *w^t* in order to save labour (irrespective of the scale of production), there remains the obvious fact that neither *with* nor *w^t* involves *þ*, and we are therefore left with a very strong pointer towards (3) as the cause of the progression from *þ^t* to *that* as seen in Hg, Trinity and El overall.

There is, in addition, a further argument that tells against (1)—that the choice of *þ^t* or *that* is primarily grammatical, not codicological. Throughout, in Hg, Trinity, and El, the scribe distinguishes in midline between the 'heavier' form *that*, which he regularly uses for the demonstrative, and the 'lighter' form *þ^t* in 'pleonastic' uses such as *when þ^t*, *whil þ^t*, *if þ^t*. It is only for the middle category of independent relative that he shows variation, and, in effect, practically the whole of his shift is due to his 'upgrading' of a proportion of the relative category from *þ^t* to *that*. Hence, if (1) were the primary factor, it would surely affect all three categories, and since it does not, it can hardly be more than secondary.

We are left, then, with a choice between (2) and (3) as the primary reason for the choice in the Trinity manuscript. Here even if (2) were to apply, it would still be significant that the scribe started with a proportion near to that of Hg but finished with a proportion nearer to that of El; at the very least it would prove that he was capable of the change, whatever the influence. Nevertheless, there are some indications against (2): first, if the different distributions in sections 1, 2, and 3 stem from the exemplar, they ought to be confirmed by other linguistic differences between these three sections, but they are not; second, this scribe's normal habit of distinguishing between different grammatical categories of *þ^t/that* should, if (2) applies, be disrupted, but it is not.

There are thus strong grounds for believing that what we see in the Trinity manuscript is the actual shift in the scribe's preference from *þ^t* to *that* and that it takes place as a result of the conflicting pressures of the exemplar and of factor (3): in section 2, the influence of the exemplar induces a high proportion of *þ*,[23] but in section 3 it is in reaction to that, and under the renewed influence of (3), that the scribe swings to the later distribution found in El. This is an attractive hypothesis and, if accepted, shows that the shift took place suddenly as a result of conflicting pressures. If, however, factor (2) is preferred as the explanation, the argument is not affected.

V

Whichever of the above explanations is favoured, the Trinity manuscript constitutes an important link in the progression from Hg to El: not only does it show the identical choice of both constants and variables, but it shows how far the shifts had proceeded, and possibly even the working of the scribe's mind (whether conscious or subconscious) when one of the shifts took place. Since the shifts seem to have taken place in consecutive batches rather than simultaneously and more gradually, it would even be possible to use the progression as a time scale: we might hazard dates of ca.1402–1404 for Hg, 1407–1409 for Trinity, and 1410–12 for El. However, at this point in the inquiry one looks rather for some other sample of this scribe's work—even if it is only a single leaf—in the hope that it might tell us more about the order of those six earlier shifts. And that is precisely what we have, in the shape of the Cecil fragment of *Troilus*, a single defective leaf in the same scribe's hand.[24] On its own, with no progression established, such a fragment would be regarded as statistically negligible and discounted, but as corroboration of an already established progression, it is invaluable. It clearly precedes Trinity, since it shows five cases of *thow* but none of *thou* and six cases of midline *þ^t^* to only one of *that*; but equally clearly it is after Hg, since *i* outnumbers *y*,[25] and *and* is unabbreviated. Then, when placed in order between Hg and Trinity, it suggests a refinement in the ordering of the shift from *-ow-* to *-ou-*: whereas in both Trinity and El the shift from *thow* to *thou* is shown to have lagged behind those of *doun* and *toun*, here it has not yet even begun, in contrast to the single instance of *toun*, which has thus preceded it. Representation of the remaining features is naturally scanty in such a fragment, but there are probably enough cases of doubled vowels to suggest that that shift has begun; the single cases of full and abbreviated *-er-* at least do not contradict the view that that shift was then in progress; and similarly its other forms do not tell against the view that the remaining changes were later: *noght* and *thoght*, crossed *h* and tailed *d* in a minority of possible instances, and *-on* three times compared with *-oun* in a single rhyme.

It is surely significant that this fragment, so far as its evidence goes, not only fits automatically at a new point (say, 1405–1406) in the progression already established but can even suggest a refinement of our knowledge of that progression. It provides the ideal corroboration that would be expected from new evidence and suggests that if yet a fifth text or fragment by this scribe were discovered it too could be expected to fall readily into place and provide still further refinements of the progression. Its significance is thus out of all proportion to its size, and it is for that reason that it is included in the following table summarising the sequence of the shifts (in this table A denotes a distribution before the shift has taken place, AB that the shift is in progress, and B that the shift has already taken place).

	Hg	Cecil Fragment	Trinity	El
y/i	A	B	B	B
ay/ey	A	B	B	B
&/and	A	B	B	B
town/toun	A	B	B	B
-er/*-er-*	A	A B	B	B
Doubled vowels	A	AB	B	B
thow/thou	A	A	B	B
h/crossed h	A	A	AB	B
þt/that	A	A	A B	B
d/tailed d	A	A	AB	B
-on/-oun	A	A	A	B
ogh/ough	A	A	A	B
with/wt	A	A	A	B

It must be stressed that the arguments here presented do not depend on the inclusion of the Cecil fragment, which is an extra bonus that we may accept or reject as we please. Since it does not carry the same statistical weight as the other three, its column above may be regarded as more hypothetical, but not necessarily in proportion to its small coverage, in view of the startling degree of corroboration and refinement that it provides.

VI

The evidence for a progression during a period of this scribe's life is thus dramatic, and, in the face of it, Ramsey's other objections lack cogency.[26] There remain his other two criteria, which relate to the greater use of final *-e* and *-n* in El. Here, as often elsewhere, Ramsey's figures for 'contrast' between Hg and El give a misleading impression, since they ignore the fact that in most cases these endings agree in both manuscripts. Then, if we are to concentrate only on the differences, it can nevertheless be shown that this scribe has the same tendency throughout: to add final *-e* and *-n* when they contravene the metre and are not present in his exemplars. This latter can be proved from the Trinity Gower, which at 4.375 reads 'Abouen alle othere men as tho': the metre clearly requires *abou*[*e*] with final *-e* elided, and the Fairfax manuscript has *Aboue*.[27]

The scribe's habitual practice can be shown by his treatment of the words for 'own' (adjective) and 'these'. It can be established statistically that his normal forms for these words throughout are *owene* and *thise*, in spite of the fact that the metre always requires *owen* and *this*.[28] It follows that when he does write *owen* and *this* in Hg he is simply taking over the metrically intended forms from his exemplar; in Trinity and El he uses his own forms in final *-e*, and there is even an instance of *owene* in the *Troilus* fragment.

In the cases of final *-e* and *-n*, therefore, it cannot be said that there is any shift in scribal practice. The difference between Hg and El here is that in Hg the scribe is likely to preserve more of Chaucer's metrically intended forms but in El to spell words according to his own habitual practice. This difference, however, is not restricted to the endings *-e* and *-n*. There are other features, of no metrical significance, for which Hg often shows relict forms from its exemplar when El has the scribe's own normal form. A typical example is the past tense of the verb *see*: there are good reasons for believing that Chaucer's own forms were *say* and *saw*,[29] and these are commoner in Hg; but the scribe's own normal form is *saugh* (with *seigh* as his earlier variant), and these, though also common in Hg, are usual in Trinity and El.

As was emphasised above, none of these cases, in aggregate, constitutes any great difference between Hg and El; overall, the scribe's practice remains the same. However, there was a considerable period—perhaps almost a decade—between the copying of the two manuscripts, and each was produced for a very different purpose, Hg being a cheaper and more makeshift volume, El a larger, more carefully planned and expensively produced one. It is not at all surprising, therefore, that the scribe should have set about each task differently, in Hg occasionally mixing the exemplar's form with his own, in El taking more care to present his own orthography consistently. To this, however, there was the paradoxical result that, being no metrist, he more often added his own unmetrical final *-e* and *-n* in the more expensive El than he had earlier done when copying Hg.

And so we return to the great array of correspondences with which we started. There are no other known Middle English texts with these linguistic profiles, and the hands are identical. If Ramsey were to insist, in spite of the progression shown here, on his theory of separate scribes, it would be logical for him to insist on four scribes for these four texts rather than two or three, for the latter course would commit him to at least some part of the progression. Let us suppose, then, for argument's sake, that they are by four separate scribes. That four men, however closely connected, should agree on the same items of spelling and show the same sets of variables, that three of them should choose to alter their proportions of variables in ascending order, and that all four of them should then fit precisely into the progression expected for a single scribe is beyond all bounds of coincidence. This is no mere example of the 'balance of probability' to which Ramsey appeals. The Trinity manuscript has provided us with evidence as near to proof as we are ever likely to get that these four texts were all written by the same scribe.

NOTES

1 R Vance Ramsey, 'The Hengwrt and Ellesmere Manuscripts of the *Canterbury Tales*: Different Scribes', *Studies in Bibliography* 35, 1982, 133–54.

2 A I Doyle and M B Parkes, 'The production of copies of the *Canterbury Tales* and *Confessio Amantis* in the early fifteenth century', in M B Parkes and A G Watson eds,

Mediæval Scribes, Manuscripts and Libraries: Essays presented to N R Ker, Scolar Press: London, 1978, 163–210.

3 Ramsey, 'Hengwrt and Ellesmere Manuscripts', p.134, with reference there made to J M Manly and E Rickert eds, *The Text of the Canterbury Tales*, UCP: Chicago, 1940, Vol I, p.558.

4 M L Samuels, 'Some Applications of Middle English Dialectology', *English Studies* 44, 1963, 81–94 (now repr in *Middle English Dialectology*, chapter 5).

5 Samuels, 'Some Applications', pp.87–88; and cf. M L Samuels, 'Chaucer's Spelling', in D Gray and E G Stanley eds, *Middle English Studies presented to Norman Davis*, OUP: Oxford, 1983, 17–37 (repr as chapter 4 above).

6 For accounts of the survey see A McIntosh, 'A New Approach to Middle English Dialectology', *English Studies* 44, 1963, 1–11 (now repr in *Middle English Dialectology*, chapter 2); and M Benskin, 'Local archives and Middle English dialects', *Journal of the Society of Archivists* 5, 1977, 500–514. See also *LALME* Vol I, General Introduction.

7 This total does not include a large number of other Middle English manuscripts that were inspected for peculiarities of language.

8 M Benskin and Margaret Laing, 'Translations and *Mischsprachen* in Middle English Manuscripts', in M Benskin and M L Samuels eds, *So Meny People Longages and Tonges: Philological Essays in Scots and Mediaeval English presented to Angus McIntosh,* MEDP: Edinburgh, 1981, 55–106; now largely reproduced in *LALME* Vol I, General Introduction 2, 2.2–2.4; 3, 2–5; and appendices.

9 Norman Davis, 'A Scribal Problem in the Paston Letters', *English and Germanic Studies* 4, 1951–1952, 31–64; Norman Davis, 'A Paston Hand', *Review of English Studies*, new series 3, 1952, 209–21.

10 M L Samuels, 'Spelling and Dialect in the Late and Post-Middle English Periods', in Benskin and Samuels, *So Meny People*, 43–54 (repr as chapter 8 below).

11 A I Doyle, 'University College, Oxford, MS 97 and Its Relationship to the Simeon Manuscript (BL Addl 22283)', in Benskin and Samuels, *So Meny People*, 265–82.

12 Benskin and Laing, 'Translations and *Mischsprachen*', p.59.

13 Benskin and Laing, 'Translations and *Mischsprachen*', pp.99–101.

14 Samuels, 'Some Applications', p.88

15 Samuels, 'Some Applications', pp.89–91.

16 Further evidence is available from the earlier MSS of Chaucer's *Troilus*, for which cf. Samuels, 'Chaucer's Spelling'.

17 Doyle and Parkes, 'The Production of Copies', pp.164, 174 ff. He is also the fourth scribe in Trinity, Cambridge R.3.2, and is therefore referred to by Doyle and Parkes as Scribe D.

18 For a fuller account of this scribe see chapters 6 and 9 below and references there cited.

19 Further evidence of such shifts can be found in other cases where one scribe wrote two MSS that survive, e.g. (1) CUL Gg 4.27 and Bodl e Musaeo 116 and (2) Bodl Bodley 423, fols. 244–351, and St John's, Cambridge 29 (B.7).

20 As even his own first set of figures shows (pp.135–6), he is omitting residues of 46 percent for *town/toun* and *at the/atte*, 37 percent for *thogh/though*, and 21 percent for *thow/thou*.

21 M L Samuels and J J Smith, 'The language of Gower', *Neuphilologische Mitteilungen* 82, 1981, 295–304 (repr as chapter 3 above).

22 Samuels, 'Chaucer's Spelling'.

23 From the Gowerian relicts in this hand, and from the greater prevalence of them in hands C, D and E, it is reasonable to assume that the exemplar was of the normal Fairfax-Stafford kind; i.e., it had midline *þat* throughout (hand A is more modern in both language and script; cf. Doyle and Parkes, 'The Production of Copies', p.168).

24 Doyle and Parkes, 'The Production of Copies', p.168.

25 For this estimate only those words that show variation in Hg and El are considered (typical examples are *lif*/*lyf* and the ending *-ie*/*-ye*).

26 For example, he makes much of the unique textual alterations in El but cannot prove that our scribe is to blame for them. As Doyle and Parkes point out ('The Production of Copies', p.186), the accuracy of copying in Hg and Trinity tells heavily against such an assumption.

27 On this addition of *-n* in both texts, see now G V Smithers, 'The Scansion of *Havelok* and the Use of ME *-en* and *-e* in *Havelok* and by Chaucer', in Gray and Stanley, *Middle English Studies*, 195–234.

28 Ramsey refers to the work of J G Southworth as if there were still uncertainty in the matter of Chaucerian metrics, but there is not. See M L Samuels, 'Chaucerian Final *-e*', *Notes and Queries* 217, 1972, 445–8 (repr as chapter 2 above); J D Burnley, 'Inflexion in Chaucer's Adjectives', *Neuphilologische Mitteilungen* 83, 1982, 169–77.

29 Samuels, 'Chaucer's Spelling'.

6 THE TRINITY GOWER D-SCRIBE AND HIS WORK ON TWO EARLY *CANTERBURY TALES* MANUSCRIPTS

J J SMITH

I

This paper takes as its starting-point a recent controversy over whether MSS BL Harley 7334 and Corpus Christi, Oxford 198 (hence Ha4 and Cp) of Chaucer's *Canterbury Tales* were written by one or two copyists. In 1978, the palaeographers Ian Doyle and Malcolm Parkes concluded that the two MSS were by one scribe, who also wrote, or was involved in writing, a large number of other late mediaeval English texts: Langland's *Piers Plowman*, Trevisa's translation of *Bartholomaeus Anglicus de proprietatibus rerum* and Gower's *Confessio Amantis*.[1] They named this copyist 'Scribe D', for the reason that his hand was the fourth of five they detected in one MS of the *Confessio*, Trinity, Cambridge R.3.2. This discovery has been generally accepted by scholars.[2]

Recently, however, Vance Ramsey has questioned this identification, in a vehemently-expressed article published in 1986.[3] The vehemence of the article derives from its being in part a response to a 1983-article by Michael Samuels[4]—itself a reply to an argument put forward by Ramsey in 1982.[5] In 1982, Ramsey drew attention to certain textual and orthographic differences between the Hengwrt and Ellesmere MSS of the *Canterbury Tales* (hence Hg and El) which, he claimed, indicated that the two texts were written by different scribes—even though the hands were otherwise 'identical'.[6] In this, he opposed Doyle and Parkes who, in their 1978 article, not only considered El and Hg to be written by the same scribe, but detected his hand in the 'Cecil Fragment' of *Troilus and Criseyde* and in the Trinity Gower beside scribe D. They called him 'scribe B'.[7] (The other scribes in the Trinity MS, A, C and E, are not the subjects of this paper).

Samuels, in his reply to Ramsey, showed that scribes frequently changed their orthographic habits, both under the influence of varying exemplars and in different personal circumstances; that the shifts in habit detected by Ramsey affected only a minor part of the orthography of this scribe, 'and then only by shifts of existing variants, not change of form';[8] and that Hg and El, along with the 'Cecil Fragment' and the 'scribe-B' stint in the Trinity Gower, were almost certainly all written by the same person. According to Samuels, the spelling-variants detected by Ramsey could be ordered sequentially to show a development of the scribe's orthography over time and under the influence of the varying exemplars he copied.

Ramsey's rejoinder re-asserted his belief that Hg and El were by different scribes, re-stating the views which he believed Samuels to have misrepresented. It is not proposed here to go over this ground once again, except incidentally; readers of the articles concerned are free to judge their respective merits. However, Ramsey in 1986 broadened his fire, turning his attention to 'scribe D' and his copying of Ha4 and Cp. For Ramsey, these MSS are also by different scribes.[9] By examining his approach in this case, I propose to show that his general methodology is basically flawed.

Nevertheless, I should state that I agree wholeheartedly with Ramsey's conclusion to his later article: 'For surely we are all united in our aims: a better understanding of the making of mediaeval books . . .'.[10] And, indeed, in questioning Ramsey's methodology it is possible to present some more positive and interesting findings.

II

Ramsey uses two tools in distinguishing his 'different' scribes:

(a) textual differences
(b) spelling-contrasts between MSS

I shall examine each in turn.

(a) textual differences

Since Samuels was accused of ignoring discussion of 'different habits in proofing and editing',[11] it seems best to start with this. Ramsey finds 'a line average (corrected for loss of lines) of 1 uncorrected unique variant per 53.81 lines' in Cp and '1 per 10.97 lines' in Ha4.[12] Furthermore, he notes a steady unwillingness to change the text in Cp against variability in Ha4. These characteristics of the MSS he considers to be the responsibility of the scribe in each case—and, because these characteristics differ, he deduces that the scribes of the MSS are different. His reasons for doing so are as follows:

> While most of the variant readings in a manuscript will have been copied from the exemplar, the percentage so derived versus those introduced by the scribe is an accurate measure of the scribe's care because he had no way of separating variants from authentic readings.[13]

The problem with Ramsey's approach is that he nowhere indicates how, in Ha4/Cp, he can distinguish the exemplar-introduced variants from his supposed scribe-introduced variants. Since the exemplars were themselves made by scribes, we can assume that they themselves possessed a degree of 'unique variation' before the Ha4/Cp scribe copied them. In other words, it is perfectly possible for the same scribe to copy different exemplars—and thus to produce textually distinct MSS.[14]

The textual problem, given Ramsey's use of compositor-studies as his model, would on its own be enough to vitiate his argument. As he indicated in 1982, '. . . while compositor-studies generally deal with different compositors working from the same copy, this study does not. (Manly and Rickert's analyses show that the use of the same exemplar for two extant manuscripts is the exception rather than the rule.)'[15] Certainly, the circumstances surrounding the textual origins of Ha4 and Cp are very different, as Doyle and Parkes—following Manly and Rickert—conclusively showed;[16] and this difference seems to favour the kind of textual variation which scribe D presents in the two MSS.

(b) spelling-differences

That exemplars could influence scribal choice of even minor spelling-variables is admitted by Ramsey:

> . . . the marked differences in the *Knight's Tale* spellings of *thou* suggest that El is copying there from an exemplar with the word spelled *thow* a larger-than-usual percentage of the time (25 out of 58 times, El spells *thow*, compared with 50 out of 457 times elsewhere.[17]

Although Ramsey did not discuss the problem of exemplar-induced spellings by reference to Ha4 and Cp, he did attempt to deal with it in 1982 with regard to El and Hg; presumably he would offer a similar explanation here. His view is, as I understand it, that the variations in accidentals should show a systematically *un*even distribution within MSS, corresponding to variation in substantive readings brought about by the textual confusions underlying the *Canterbury Tales* tradition.[18] Even this, however, does not follow; as Samuels puts it, 'one could postulate any number of intermediate exemplars, all of which preserved the stemma confusions, but which—at least in the copy antecedent to El—had had all their inconsistencies in spelling homogenized by the translation process so frequent in Middle English.'[19]

Leaving aside, for the moment, the question of exemplar-induced spellings, we should now address another problem raised by Ramsey's arguments: the question as to whether spelling-variation is allowable within a single scribe's orthographic repertoire. In 1982, Ramsey argued as follows:

> The question . . . is not variability (which is inevitable) but *tendency*: if the same scribe did copy the many thousands of lines in each manuscript, then whatever the reasons for his variations in spelling, his tendency to use a particular grapheme for a particular sound or sound-combination should be apparent in any very large count.[20]

As I understand it, Ramsey's argument is not that scribes persistently use single spelling-forms, but that the proportions of one variable to another for a particular word is fixed within a scribe's repertoire. Thus he would argue, for example, that

Scribe X *always* uses 80 percent *þ^t^* to 20 percent *that*, whereas Scribe Y *always* uses 60 percent *þ^t^* to 40 percent *that*, and that these proportions never change, whatever the circumstances:

> I believe that any professional scribe copying texts in English every working day of his life, year after year, would *fix* his habits in registering accidentals and substantives just as he would fix his habits in the way he made his letters with a pen, habits which he would tend to impose upon the texts which he was copying.[21]

In fact, such changes—in professional scribes—are well-attested. In a portion of his paper not addressed by Ramsey in his rejoinder, Samuels did discuss this problem, and drew attention to a number of MSS in which such shifts took place.[22] However, given the way in which the debate has continued, it seems best to look here at a study not derived from the Middle English Dialect Survey: Hamer's work on the spellings of the fifteenth-century professional scribe, Ricardus Franciscus.[23]

The hand of Ricardus has been identified in a number of fifteenth-century MSS, viz.:

Bodl Ashmole 764
Bodl Laud Misc 570
University Coll, Oxford 85
Huntington, Cal., 932
BL Harley 4775
New York, Pierpont Morgan Libr M.126[24]

Harley 4775, a MS of the *Gilte Legende*, is a direct copy of Bodl Douce 372,[25] and Hamer used this discovery to compare Ricardus' spelling-habits with those of this original. He summarised his findings as follows:

> . . . comparison of [Harley 4775] with [Douce 372] shows at once what a very close and accurate copyist Ricardus was. He makes a very few small corrections if they are absolutely obvious, such as completing a word left unfinished at the end of a line, but generally he does not rectify even blatant errors . . . In writing that 'he was a professional scribe who copied extremely faithfully, so that his text is likely to retain even some of the dialectal forms of his exempla', Auvo Kurvinen understated the position. Apart from such points as his rejection of *þ* and frequent avoidance of *ȝ*, he copies most words exactly, even if they appear in a variety of forms. Thus *hundreth*, *hundrith*, *hundrid*, *hundretȝ*; *eyen*, *yeen*, *yen*, *eien*, *eyȝen*; *nobul*, *nobil*, *nobill*, *nobille*, *noble* are all copied. But a number of other words which appear in [Douce 372] with various spellings, while often copied by Ricardus in the forms in [Douce 372], are also quite frequently changed to particular spellings which are so consistently used that they must represent his own preferences or 'dialect'.[26]

The Douce MS was copied by four hands; Ricardus' spellings reflect the spelling-variation between these hands. The key feature for our purposes is that Ricardus is a professional scribe, 'copying texts in English every working day of his life'; yet he still faithfully reflects many features of spelling-variation in his exemplars.

Many similar examples of scribal behaviour could be given; a classic, for instance, is the spelling-system of the Caligula MS of *The Owl and the Nightingale*, distinguished by Atkins in 1922.[27] Such examples are, surely, enough to disprove Ramsey's assertion that scribes cannot change their habits—let alone that variable-proportions are fixed within a scribe's repertoire of spellings.

III

Both Ramsey's arguments, therefore, are shown to be flawed. How does this affect his contention with regard to Ha4 and Cp? How did the spelling-variations in these MSS arise? I propose to introduce a positive note into this article by laying out my own findings on the spelling-systems of the two MSS.[28]

Ramsey complained that Samuels had not demonstrated his methodology,[29] even though full citation was given to the literature on the relationship between spelling and textual transmission in Middle English.[30] It is for this reason that this portion of the critique begins with a methodological outline.

Data were collected using the questionnaires devised by the Middle English Dialect Survey.[31] Extensive tranches of text in each MS were analysed; passages between each tranche were read through for forms not recorded there. All analyses, with counts, are fully published in my thesis;[32] considerations of space make their full presentation here impossible. However, a model of the questionnaire used is given in the notes.[33] It should be emphasised that the questionnaire was simply a convenient method of gathering a great deal of information, and had, necessarily, to be comparatively selective; every word in the MSS—and every form of every word—has been scrutinised as possible linguistic evidence,[34] orthography being as much a facet of language as phonology or syntax.[35]

It should, perhaps, be mentioned that Ramsey's doubts as to the validity of dialectal expertise in such studies are misplaced;[36] for instance, of the ten orthographic characteristics distinguishing Ha4 and Cp which he chooses to examine,[37] at least six are of dialectal significance.[38] I shall be returning to these spelling-contrasts later.

Any Middle English copyist of works not composed by himself must belong to one of three categories of scribe distinguished by McIntosh and later re-stated by Benskin and Laing.[39] A scribe copying an exemplar can do one of three things:

A He may leave the language [of his exemplar] more or less unchanged. This appears to happen only somewhat rarely.

B He may convert it into his own kind of language, making innumerable modifications to the orthography, the morphology and the vocabulary. This happens commonly.

C He may do something somewhere between A and B. This also happens commonly.[40]

Examination of Ha4 and Cp shows that they present linguistic mixtures—so-called *Mischsprachen*—made up of forms which do not cohere in any one dialect area, representing the linguistic interventions of subsequent scribes on the archetypal language of the text. Assigning these 'layers' of language to particular scribes is a complex business in its details, but basically simple in conception. An hypothetical example might be as follows: A scribe writes three MSS (x, y and z) with different textual histories. This scribe was of McIntosh's Type C, and thus produced a mixture of his own forms and forms from his exemplars. Thus the linguistic mixtures in the MSS appear as follows:

MS	x	y	z
Linguistic mixture	West Midland + North	East Anglian + North	Kentish + North

Here we might postulate the Northern layer, common to all three MSS, as the scribe's input.

However, this is (admittedly) a simplified hypothetical example. Many problems to do with the relationship between scribe and exemplar are to be found, and have been exhaustively discussed by Benskin and Laing.[41] The concepts enunciated by them have been adopted here. According to Benskin and Laing, analysis of a *Mischsprache* begins by finding a location which accounts for the greatest number of forms in a given MS. 'Recalcitrant' forms are sifted out, and then subjected to the same process, in order to find the location which will account for the greatest number of *those* forms. But, as Benskin and Laing point out,

> . . . only as long as we assume that the number of geographical subsets is small rather than large does the conclusion [that this is a sound approach] hold. Nevertheless, there is good reason to believe that multiple contamination is not common: it takes only one scribe, who habitually translates from the dialect of an exemplar into his own, to break the chain of communication, to convert the language of the text into a single and internally consistent dialect . . . Such scribes seem to have been a majority in the later ME period . . . Similarly . . . the more contributions we postulate for which we do not have decisive evidence, the more likely it is that in our reconstruction we shall be mistaken.[42]

IV

When this methodology is employed, there would appear to be a number of sets of linguistic elements in the Cp *Mischsprache*:

(a) There are many features which resemble the parallel form in El/Hg—although, interestingly, a number of these are minor variants in Cp. Examples include: *swich(e)* 'SUCH', *þough* 'THOUGH', *neiþer* 'NEITHER', (cf.El *neither*), *þey* 'THEY' (cf.El *they*), *hem* 'THEM', *if* 'IF', *nat* 'NOT', *many* 'MANY', *saugh* 'SAW' (vb), *þurgh* 'THROUGH' (cf.El *thurgh*), *yeue(n)* 'GIVEN', *hire* 'THEIR'. A number of other forms in Cp, although not found in El, are to be found in other contemporary London texts: *þese* 'THESE', *such(e)* 'SUCH', *here* 'THEIR', *eny* 'ANY', *þeigh* 'THOUGH', for example, all appear in the London texts printed by Chambers and Daunt.[43]

(b) Another set of forms include *vche* 'EACH', perhaps *boþen* 'BOTH', *nough* and *nouȝ* 'NOT', *mon*, 'MAN', persistent OE *y* in *u*, in *fuyr* 'FIRE' etc., and the rhyming pair *writynk* 'WRITING': *þink* 'THING'. With these forms might cohere: *ar* 'ERE', *meche* 'MUCH', *seluer* 'SILVER', *-ur*, *nouþer* and *Noyþer* 'NEITHER' and, even, *werld* 'WORLD'. Middle English dialect maps show that these forms cohere in the SW Midlands.[44]

(c) However, *werld* is much more common in Northern and Eastern areas, and there are traces of East Anglian dialect in the text. Diagnostically East Anglian is *drynclyng* (n.) 'DROWNING', beside *schat* 'SHALT'. Other forms could be classified with these: *boþen* 'BOTH' is found in East Anglia as well as in the West Midlands, and the forms *say* 'SAW', *ony* 'ANY', *þey* 'THOUGH', the frequent *-ij-* form in *wijf* 'WIFE,', *lijf* 'LIFE' and the tendency to use *y* in words like 'YET' rather than *ȝ* all cohere in East Anglia.[45]

(d) A Northern layer is just possible, indicated by *ilke* 'EACH', *ware* 'WERE', *þem* 'THEM', *þer* and *þair* 'THEIR', *displeses* 'DISPLEASES', *til* and *till* 'TO', *felynglik* 'FEELINGLY', *haly* 'HOLY'. Even though their heartland is in the North, most of these forms are recorded sporadically in the Midlands and, if the principle of minimising possible layers is strictly adhered to, could be accommodated in either the SW Midlands or East Anglian layers already identified. *Haly* 'HOLY' is hard to accommodate in such areas, although it is quite common in reduced-stress situations, e.g. *halichirche*.[46]

Have a look for some of these?

(e) *oughne* 'OWN' (adj.). At this date, this feature is mainly Kentish; a 'recalcitrant' form, which does not cohere with any of the other sets of forms already distinguished in this text,[47] it will be discussed further below. It appears here beside *owne* etc.

Similarly, Ha4 presents a dialectally-mixed text, another *Mischsprache*. At least four sets of forms can be distinguished:

(a) A number of forms in El/Hg also appear in Ha4, e.g. *any* 'ANY', *agayn* 'AGAIN', *er* 'ERE', *þey* 'THEY' (cf.El *they*), *nat* 'NOT', *eyen* 'EYES', *saugh* 'SAW', *þurgh* 'THROUGH' (cf.El *thurgh*), *togidere(s)* 'TOGETHER', *swich* 'SUCH'.

(b) A South-West Midland element in the language of Ha4 is strongly-marked: *þeof* 'THIEF', *eorþe* 'EARTH', *nough* 'NOT', *ar* 'ERE', *seih*, *sawh*, and *seyh* 'SAW', *-ur*, *-us* and *-ud*, *furst* 'FIRST', *silf* 'SELF', *yhen* 'EYES', and many examples of OE *y* in *u*, *uy*, e.g. *fuyr* 'FIRE', *put* 'PIT'.[48]

(c) Some Northernisms form a separate element, much more strongly marked than in Cp: *til* 'TO', *þeir* 'THEIR', *bathe* 'BOTH', *mekil* 'MUCH', *-and* pres.part. inflexion, 3rd pres.sg. inflexion in *-s* (e.g. *comes*, *writes*, *bathis*). It is possible that this Northern input is responsible for Ha4's having more examples of *call-* 'CALL' (vs. *clepe*), *wil* 'WILL' (vs. *wol*) and *ony* 'ANY' (vs. *eny*, *any*) than Cp. It could also be responsible for the wholesale loss of Chaucerian final *-e* in this MS.[49]

(d) A Kentish element is indicated by *oughne* 'OWN' (adj.), possibly supported by *hiere* 'HEAR' and *þerwhiles þat* 'WHILE', but these latter could also be assigned to the better-established SW Midland input already indicated.[50]

In both MSS, it should be stressed, the majority of forms are commonly found in the Southern Midlands, many of them invariable between the MSS. Thus both commonly have *sche* 'SHE', *which* 'WHICH', *schal* (sg.) 'SHALL', *wolde* 'WOULD', *þough* 'THOUGH', *might* 'MIGHT' (vb.), *whan* 'WHEN', *held* 'HELD', *but* 'BUT', *self* 'SELF', *world* 'WORLD', *lasse* 'LESS' etc. This list could be greatly extended.[51]

If we now extrapolate from the hypothetical model given above, then we can reconstruct the linguistic origins of the two MSS as follows:

i) Group (a) in both MSS most probably stems from the archetypal Chaucerian tradition.[52]
ii) The Northernisms in Cp are weakly marked, and should probably be merged with the East Anglian layer in that MS. They are much more strongly marked in Ha4, and make up there a distinctive layer, spread throughout the MS.
iii) The East Anglian layer is peculiar to Cp.
iv) Common to both MSS are the strong SW Midland layer and the solitary Kentish form, *oughne* 'OWN' (adj.).

At first, this seems to produce a puzzling situation; the scribe would appear to be a SW Midlander into whose repertoire a stray Kenticism, *oughne*, has somehow crept. This explanation, however, becomes less unlikely when Ha4 and Cp are compared with the other MSS copied by Scribe D.

V

Scribe D's hand has so far been recognised in 12 MSS, viz.:

Trinity, Cambridge R.3.2 (Gower, *Confessio Amantis*; D is responsible for quires 9, 15 to 19, and parts of 14);
University Libr, London V.88 (Langland, *Piers Plowman* 'C-text', *olim* Ilchester MS);
BL Addl 27944 (Trevisa's translation of *Bartholomaeus Anglicus de proprietatibus rerum*; D is responsible for fols. 2–7v, 96–335v);
Bodl Bodley 902 (Gower, *Confessio Amantis*; D is responsible for fols. 2–16v);
Corpus Christi, Oxford, B.67 (Gower, *Confessio Amantis*);
Christ Church, Oxford 148 (Gower, *Confessio Amantis*);
Columbia University Libr, NY, Plimpton 265 (Gower, *Confessio Amantis*);
BL Egerton 1991, (Gower, *Confessio Amantis*);

Bodl Bodley 294 (Gower, *Confessio Amantis*);
Princeton, University Libr, Robert H Taylor MS (Gower, *Confessio Amantis*, *olim* Rosenbach 369, *olim* Phillipps 8192; D is responsible for fols. 7r–190r);
The two MSS of the *Canterbury Tales* already discussed (Ha4 and Cp).[53]

Examination of the language of each of these MSS makes D's behaviour much more explicable. In the Trevisa and Langland texts we find a mixture similar to that in the Chaucer MSS: layers of probably archetypal and distinctively SW Midland forms, with fragmentary indications of other layers.[54] In both MSS the lone Kenticism *oughne* appears. With the Gower MSS, the archetypal language of the tradition can be identified in detail.[55] All these MSS contain a mixture of archetypal and SW Midland forms; some contain a few Northern relicts.[56] Scribe D evidently made a specialty of copying MSS of Gower, and it is from the Gower tradition that *oughne* comes. *-g(h)-* forms for this item (e.g. *oghne*, *ougne*, *ogne*, *oughne* etc, as opposed to *owne*, *owen* etc) are a characteristic feature of the spelling-systems of Gowerian MSS, stemming from Gower's own practice for this item.[57] The form presumably entered D's repertoire through repeated copying, passively at first and later, when copying non-Gowerian texts, actively.

Once *oughne* has been set aside, D's dialectal origins become more apparent. His co-operation with a known person, Thomas Hoccleve, in the construction of the Trinity Gower (Hoccleve is Scribe E in the nomenclature of Doyle and Parkes) suggests that he shared Hoccleve's place of residence, London.[58] But his persistent SW Midland forms suggest that he was an immigrant to the capital from that area. Sporadic forms in his MSS such as *huyre* 'HEAR', *-ww*(-) in 'BLOW', 'JAW' etc, the rare *e*-prefix in past participles, *þouh* 'THOUGH', *silf* 'SELF', *nough* and *nouȝ* 'NOT', *hegh* 'HIGH', *seih* etc 'SAW', *-leche* for '-LY', *-ur* in words like 'AFTER', OE *y* reflected in *u*, *uy* (e.g. *fuyr* 'FIRE'), *ȝongþe* 'YOUTH', *eorþe* 'EARTH' indicate a probable origin in W Worcestershire.[59]

ITEM	Scribe D's copies of: Trevisa	Langland	Chaucer	Gower
'THESE'	þese	þese, þise	þese, þise	þese
'SUCH'	such(e)	such(e)	such(e)	such(e)
'ANY'	eny	eny	eny	eny
'MUCH'	moche	moche	moche	moche
'AGAIN'	aȝein	aȝein	aȝein	aȝein
'YET'	ȝit	ȝit	ȝit	ȝit
'TOGETHER'	togidre	togidre	togidre	togidre
'EYE(S)'	yhe(n)	yhe(n)	yhe(n)	yhe(n)
pres.part. inflexion	-yng(e)	-yng(e), -ing	-yng(e)	-end(e), -ing, -yng
'THROUGH'	þurgh, þorugh	þurgh, þorgh, thurgh	þurgh	þurgh
'HEAR'	hier-, he(e)r-	her-	hier-, he(e)r-	hier-, he(e)r-

However, it should be emphasised that the markedly SW Midland forms, in all of D's MSS, are comparatively rare. In the table on page 59, a selection of D's characteristic forms is given in each of the traditions he copies. Main forms only are given, for reasons of space;[60] sporadic and rarer forms have been excluded. In this table, several forms persistently appear in all or in a majority of the traditions within which scribe D is copying. Such forms as *þese*, *such(e)*, *eny*, *moche*, *aȝein*, *ȝit*, *togidre*, *yhe(n)*, *-yng*, *þurgh*, *hier-/he(e)r-* may, therefore, be considered to make up scribe D's 'basic repertoire'. However, there is a complicating factor. The table above might be compared with the following listing of the equivalent forms in the archetypal languages of the traditions cited. Again, only main forms are given, for reasons of space:[61]

ITEM	Trevisa	Langland	Chaucer	Gower
'THESE'	þues,þeos, þes,þeus	this(e)	thise	þese
'SUCH'	such,soche	suche	swich	such(e)
'ANY'	eny,any	eny	any	eny
'MUCH'	moche, muche,	moche	moche, muche	moche
'AGAIN'	aȝe(ne(s))	aȝe(y)nes	agayns	aȝein
'YET'	ȝut	ȝet, ȝut	yet	ȝit
'TOGETHER'	togedres	togedre(s)	togidre(s)	togedre(s)
'EYE(S)'	yȝen	yes	eyen	yhe(n)
pres.part. inflexion	yng(e)	yng	-yng(e)	-ende
'THROUGH'	þorouȝ	thorw	thurgh	þurgh
'HERE'	hure	here	heere	hiere

What is plain from a comparison of these two tables is that the forms which make up scribe D's 'basic repertoire' coincide most frequently with the forms in the archetypal Gowerian tradition.

There would appear to be two possible explanations for this phenomenon. Either scribe D has learnt the Gowerian forms, and spread them to other traditions, or the forms correspond coincidentally. The answer would seem to be a combination of the two. The great majority of forms in D's repertoire, and all the forms in his 'basic repertoire', have a widespread distribution in Middle English.[62] They could even be assigned to the SW Midland layer already identified—and, perhaps, given the principle of minimising layers, should be. The only forms in D's repertoire which cannot be explained in these terms are the form *oughne* 'OWN', already discussed above, and a few relict forms from individual traditions.

Central, however, to an understanding of scribe D's behaviour is the concept of *constraint*. The concept has been defined thus:

> A scribe follows his exemplar in such a way as to suppress altogether some of his habitual forms, and to alter substantially the relative frequencies of forms that are

> functionally equivalent. Except for the occasional relict, forms alien to the scribal dialect are not reproduced.[63]

To give a brief hypothetical example: a scribe has two forms for the item 'IT' in his repertoire, *it* and *itt*. On one occasion, however, he has to copy an exemplar which contains only *itt*. *Itt* is familiar to the scribe, and he reproduces it whenever it appears; and, if this were the only evidence we had as to the scribe's usage, we would not know that *it* was in his repertoire at all. D's behaviour is comparable. With the exception of *oughne*, the 'Gowerian' forms D selects are also his 'own' forms, widely available in the Southern Midlands; and there are 'Gowerian' forms he rejects. For instance, D very rarely reproduces Gowerian *togedre* 'TOGETHER'; his preferred form for this item is almost always with medial *-i-*, *-y-*. The form with *-e-* was almost certainly in his exemplars of the *Confessio Amantis*; the fact that he chose not to reproduce what was a very common S Midland form of the word[64] shows that it was definitely not in his repertoire.

Scribe D's linguistic behaviour, therefore, is the result of a complex interrelationship between his exemplars and his dialectal origins. Despite the similarities, it is unlikely that he learnt forms from his Gower MSS, other than *oughne*; but it is possible that repeated copying of Gowerian forms reinforced them as variables so that they also appear more frequently than might have been expected in his copies of Trevisa, Langland and Chaucer.

VI

Constraint, therefore, explains the contrasts between Ha4 and Cp tabulated by Ramsey.[65] Moreover, a number of Ramsey's contrasts can be explained in terms of the dialect layers underlying scribe D's copying: *ȝ* in Ha4 where Cp has *y*; Ha4's *lyf*, *wyf* against Cp's *lijf*, *wijf*; *-e* in Cp where Ha4 has -ø.[66] However, there are other interesting distinctions which Ramsey's table, by restricting itself to contrasts and giving no information about texts beyond the *Man of Law's Tale*,[67] does not reveal.

Ramsey believes that the spelling-habits of professional scribes are 'fixed';[68] but examination of Ha4's spellings alone shows that this cannot be the case. In Ha4, there are a whole series of changes in spellings for particular items during the course of copying. Some change erratically; others are more concentrated in particular areas of the MS. The appearances of the forms for 'WILL' demonstrate the first of these. In tranches of text analysed from the *General Prologue*, the *Miller's Tale*, the *Man of Law's Tale* and the *Wife of Bath's Prologue and Tale*, *wol* is the dominant form with *wil* as, at most, a sporadic variant. In the *Merchant's Tale*, *wil*, however, becomes the dominant form; but, in the *Franklin's Tale*, *wol* displaces *wil*, and it is still the majority form in the *Canon's Yeoman Tale*, although *wil* has increased as a proportion of all the forms for this item. In the *Pardoner's Tale*, the two forms are approximately equal in number but, by the *Shipman's Tale*, *wil* has once again become only a minor variant. In the *Manciple's Tale*, *wil* is fairly frequent; in the *Parson's Tale*, it is only sporadic.[69] Similar confusions can be seen, for instance, in the forms for 'YET',

'AGAIN' and 'ANY'.[70] Scribe D was plainly familiar with both *wil* and *wol*, as the appearance of the forms in his other MSS shows, and it would appear that the appearance of one or other in his exemplar activated the corresponding form in his repertoire. Such confusion sits well with the picture given by Manly and Rickert of exemplars for this MS—or for the exemplar for this MS—being brought together from various sources.[71]

One group of shifting forms, however, does seem to correlate in distribution in the MS. Dean, following Furnivall, noticed that 'early in the MS there are *-ud*, *-us* endings . . . giving way to *-id*, *-is* endings'.[72] The *-us*, *-ud* and the related *-ur* endings are generally Western,[73] and it would at first seem logical to group them with the SW Midland element already identified. However, other SW Midland forms—such as *fuyr* 'FIRE' etc—persist fairly steadily throughout the MS, whereas *-us*, *-ud* and *aftur* 'AFTER' are not found after the *Knight's Tale*, and *-ur* is only sporadic after then.[74] Similar patterns are followed by the forms for 'COULD', 'ERE', 'THEY' and 'NOT'.[75] It may be significant that Manly and Rickert noticed a change in the palaeographical make-up of Ha4 between the *Man of Law's Tale* and the *Wife of Bath's Tale*. Manly and Rickert noted that rubricated page-headings and the systematic use of *incipits* and *explicits* begin only after this point in the MS.[76]

Although the shifts in Cp are less violent than in Ha4, they form a similar general pattern. One set changes gradually; at the beginning of the MS the forms are frequent, but they become progressively less so, finally disappearing altogether. Another set appears suddenly, late in the MS, and is comparatively frequent there. Thus, in Cp, D appears to use more *ȝ*-spellings in words like 'YET', 'AGAIN' rather than *y/g/gh* as copying proceeds. There is a tendency for *wil* 'WILL' to become progressively less frequent in the MS, although it is already a minor variant at the outset. At the beginning of the MS, *þei* is the preferred form for 'THEY', but it becomes an increasingly rare variant, finally being replaced by *þey*; a parallel development appears to take place with the other, much rarer, forms for this item in the MS, *þai* and *þay*. *þai* appears only early in the MS.[77]

None of these shifts is especially dialectally significant. The forms which appear late in the MS, however, include two markedly dialectal features, the forms for 'GIVEN' and 'MUCH', *ȝoue(n)* and *meche*. Most interestingly, a number of *ȝoue(n)* -type forms appear at the same place in La as in Cp, and also in the Petworth House MS (Pw). Such forms were evidently in the common ancestor for Cp, La and Pw, and throw some light on their textual relationships.[87]

The relationship between spelling and textual affiliation, therefore, is a close one in this case— and deserves further investigation. As I have indicated elsewhere, 'we are not yet in that fortunate position where we can afford to neglect any source of information which might suggest relationships between manuscripts'.[79] Examination of the spellings of the Chaucer tradition, along the lines of work on the Gower MSS which I have treated elsewhere,[80] seems likely to be fruitful.

However, the main point of this article has surely been made. Scribe D's spellings in the Chaucer MSS can be explained fully, in line with the most recent developments in the analysis of *Mischsprachen*. Ramsey's arguments, from textual differences and spelling contrasts between MSS, can be shown to be logically flawed, and to ignore strong contrary findings. The weight of the evidence, notably the idiosyncratic mixture of West Worcestershire forms and the learnt form, *oughne*, combined with the 'identity' of the two hands, makes it as conclusive as it is ever likely to be that the same scribe wrote Ha4 and Cp, and that that scribe was scribe D.[81]

NOTES

1 A I Doyle and M B Parkes, 'The production of copies of the *Canterbury Tales* and the *Confessio Amantis* in the early fifteenth century', in M B Parkes and A G Watson eds, *Mediæval scribes, manuscripts and libraries: essays presented to N R Ker*, Scolar Press: London, 1978, 163–210, pp.174–82 and *passim*.

2 E.g. N F Blake, *The Textual Tradition of the Canterbury Tales*, Arnold: London, 1985.

3 R V Ramsey, 'Palaeography and Scribes of Shared Training', *Studies in the Age of Chaucer* 8, 1986, 107–44.

4 M L Samuels, 'The Scribe of the Hengwrt and Ellesmere Manuscript of *The Canterbury Tales*', *Studies in the Age of Chaucer* 5, 1983, 49–65 (repr as chapter 5 above).

5 R V Ramsey, 'The Hengwrt and Ellesmere Manuscript of *The Canterbury Tales*: Different Scribes', *Studies in Bibliography* 35, 1982, 133–54.

6 The matter as to whether Ramsey considers the hands in Hg and El 'identical' has become controversial (see Ramsey, 'Palaeography', pp.109–10), and therefore deserves some discussion. In 1986, Ramsey writes thus:

> At the very beginning of his article Samuels offered a reading of my position quite at variance with it:
>
> > He [Ramsey] admits that the hands are 'identical', and states that they are so because his two scribes received identical training. He quotes no parallels for such a phenomenon, and it is doubtful whether he could do so for any but Chancery-trained scribes. Suffice it here to say that he is not arguing with the palaeographers: he has conceded them their case. [Samuels, 'The Scribe of the Hengwrt and Ellesmere MSS', p.49 (now p.38 above)]
>
> One very real difficulty posed by Samuels's article is that such assertions neither quote nor give page references. I believe, however, that the following is the statement alluded to: 'The scribes of Hg and El must have trained and worked in the same shop, a point to be returned to in connection with their identical-appearing hands.' [Ramsey, 'Hengwrt and Ellesmere MSS', p.137] Any concession that the hands are in fact identical would have made the whole article rather silly, of course; and, whatever the case for my poor self, I should wonder at the willingness of the distinguished editor of *Studies in Bibliography* to publish such a thing. On the contrary, I called the hands in Hg and El 'identical-*appearing*' (italics added in deference to the judgements of A I Doyle and M B Parkes, distinguished palaeographers . . . (p.109)

But, in 1982, we find Ramsey writing as follows: 'The Hg scribe's total rejection of *elles* is the unique exception in this study (he must know that it *is* an option his *identical hand* [my italics] showing him to be working in the same shop with the El scribes)' (p.139); 'The answer to how the handwriting of different scribes can be in effect *identical* [my italics] . . .' (p.144); 'The point of training for such *identity of hand* [my italics] . . .' (p.144). It seems disingenuous, to say the least, to disclaim a term used so frequently. Samuels cannot be legitimately blamed for failing to give a reference for so often-quoted a claim; any readers of Ramsey, 'Hengwrt and Ellesmere MSS'—which, of course, Samuels refers to—can do so for themselves. It should be noted that Ramsey, 'Palaeography' views Scribe D's MSS in similar terms: 'If the Ha4 scribe *shares his hand* [my italics] with the Cp scribe . . . ' (p.131).

7 Doyle and Parkes, 'The production of copies', pp.170–3 and *passim*.

8 Samuels, 'The Scribe of the Hengwrt and Ellesmere Manuscript', p.56 (pp.42–3 above).

9 Ramsey, 'Palaeography', pp.126–34.

10 Ramsey, 'Palaeography', p.144.

11 Ramsey, 'Palaeography', p.126.

12 Ramsey, 'Palaeography', p.131.

13 Ramsey, 'Palaeography', p.130.

14 The textual problem in El and Hg was addressed by Samuels, 'The Scribe of the Hengwrt and Ellesmere MSS', p.63 note 26 (now p.50 above).

15 Ramsey, 'Hengwrt and Ellesmere MSS', p.137. Ramsey does not discuss this problem with reference to Ha4/Cp, but attempted to deal with it for El/Hg. In 1986, he summed up the situation as follows:

> The real potential difficulty for my study was from the possible complications posed by the influence of the varying exemplars used in copying Hg and El. Hinman and others could take for granted that the different compositors set up the First Folio from shared texts; for most of the Hengwrt and Ellesmere manuscripts, I could not. Hence my relief to discover the Manly-Rickert judgment that the scribes had shared the exemplar for *The Friar's Tale* and *The Summoner's Tale* through line 1990 [*sic*; line 1991 in Ramsey 'Hengwrt and Ellesmere MSS']; as noted above, a third chart demonstrated that the [spelling]-contrasts obtained whether the exemplars were the same or very different, reassuring proof that the variations stemmed from the scribes themselves rather than from their exemplars. (Ramsey, 'Palaeography', p.119).

An interesting point is that Ramsey is much more definite in 1986 about Manly/Rickert's views on the 'common exemplar' than he was in 1982: 'While Manly and Rickert stop short of affirming that Hg and El used the same exemplar up to line 1991 . . . ' (Ramsey 'Hengwrt and Ellesmere MSS', p.142). This is an important reservation. The problem not addressed by Ramsey in either of his articles can perhaps best be demonstrated diagrammatically. For this portion of the *Canterbury Tales*, Manly and Rickert assume a common ancestor, O, for El and Hg (see J Manly and E Rickert, *The Text of the Canterbury Tales*, UCP: Chicago, 1940, e.g. Vol I, p.150):

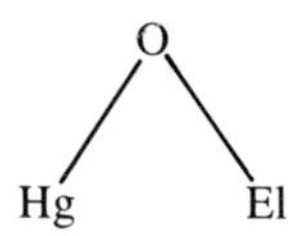

But textual critics are generally careful not to rule out intermediate exemplars appearing between O and *either* El, *or* Hg, *or* both, thus:

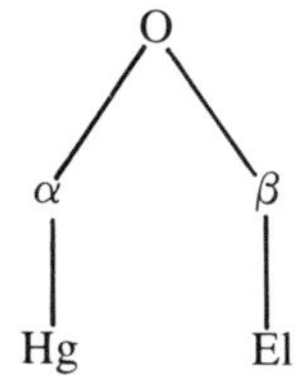

In 1982, Ramsey is careful enough simply to refer to the 'closeness' of these MSS at this point (Ramsey, 'Hengwrt and Ellesmere MSS', p.142). Such intermediate exemplars as α and/or β could easily have introduced any of the spelling-contrasts Ramsey detects.

16 Ramsey, 'Palaeography' also introduces MS BL Lansdowne 851 into his discussion. Although 'it was probably copied from the same exemplar as Cp itself' (Ramsey, 'Palaeography', p.128), Manly and Rickert indicate that 'La is inaccurately copied and is obviously much edited' (Manly and Rickert, *Canterbury Tales*, Vol I, p.306). A detailed comparison of spellings between Cp and La would have been interesting, but Ramsey does not attempt it (I have made a preliminary study in *Studies in the language of some manuscripts of Gower's Confessio Amantis,* Diss. PhD, Glasgow, 1985, pp.227–31). Since the point of Ramsey's article was to compare Cp and Ha4, with their very different textual affiliations, the reasons for including La in the table are unclear to me.

17 Ramsey, 'Hengwrt and Ellesmere MSS', p.137.

18 Ramsey, 'Hengwrt and Ellesmere MSS', p.142.

19 Samuels, 'The Scribe of the Hengwrt and Ellesmere MSS', p.58 (now p.44 above); and see M Benskin and M Laing, 'Translations and *Mischsprachen* in Middle English Manuscripts', in M Benskin and M L Samuels eds, *So meny people longages and tonges: philological essays in Scots and mediaeval English presented to Angus McIntosh*, MEDP: Edinburgh, 55–106, *passim.*

20 Ramsey, 'Hengwrt and Ellesmere MSS', p.139.

21 Ramsey, 'Palaeography', p.124.

22 Samuels, 'The Scribe of the Hengwrt and Ellesmere MSS', p.51 and references there cited (now p.39 above).

23 R Hamer, 'Spellings of the fifteenth-century scribe Ricardus Franciscus', in E G Stanley and D Gray eds, *Five Hundred Years of Words and Sounds: a Festschrift for Eric Dobson*, Brewer: Cambridge, 63–73. I am grateful to Dr Margaret Laing for drawing my attention to the appropriateness of this article to my argument.

24 Hamer, 'Ricardus Franciscus', pp.63–9. MS New York, Pierpont Morgan Library, M.126, a text of Gower's *Confessio Amantis*, has been added to Hamer's list. I am grateful to Jeremy Griffiths for notice of this MS.

25 Hamer, 'Ricardus Franciscus'. p.69.

26 Hamer, 'Ricardus Franciscus', pp.69–70.

27 J W H Atkins ed., *The Owl and the Nightingale*, CUP: Cambridge, 1922, esp. pp.xxix–xxxi; also p.187, n. 1 and references there cited.

28 What follows is a shortened account of material presented in chapter 4 of Smith, *Studies*.

29 Ramsey, 'Palaeography', p.126.

30 Samuels, 'The Scribe of the Hengwrt and Ellesmere MSS', pp.50–51 and references there cited (now p.39 above).

31 For an account, see *LALME* Vol I, pp.2–38.

32 Smith, *Studies*, Vol II.

33 Forms for the following items were collected from tranches throughout the text: 'THE', 'HE', 'HIS', 'SHE', 'HER', 'IT', 'THEY', 'THEM', 'THEIR', 'SUCH', 'WHICH', 'EACH', 'MANY', 'MAN', 'ANY', 'MUCH', 'ARE', 'IS', 'DOES', 'GOES', contracted 3rd present sg. verbs, 'SHALL', 'SHALT', 'SHOULD', 'WOULD', 'WILL', 'ASK', 'RUN', 'WITH(-)', 'AFTER', 'THEN', 'THAN', '(AL)THOUGH', 'IF', '(N)EITHER . . . (N)OR', 'SELF', *thilke* etc., 'AGAIN(ST)', *siþen* etc., 'ERE', 'YET', '(W)HENCE', 'THITHER', 'WHITHER', 'WHILE', 'TOGETHER', 'BEFORE', past participle prefixes, 'WERE', OE *hw*-reflexes, 'NOT', 'EYE(S)', 'HIGH', 'WORLD(LY)', 'THINK', 'WORK', present participle endings, 'I', *-es/-is/-us*, *-ed/-id/-ud*, 'LITTLE', 'MIGHT', 'THROUGH', 'LESS', 'WHEN', 'FIRST', 'YOUTH', 'CHURCH', 'SILVER', 'EVIL', 'HUNDRED', 'OWN' (adj.), 'DID', 'STEAD', 'LET', 'WAS', 'GAVE', 'GIVEN', 'HELD', 'SAW', 'CAME', *clepe/calle* etc., 'HEAR', Adv. '-LY', 'WHETHER', OE *y*-reflexes, 'BUT', 'BETWEEN', 'HOLY', 'OLD', 'LONG', 'PEOPLE', 'WIFE', 'LIFE', *-er/-ir/-ur*, *ȝ/y*, 'UPON', 'PENCE', 'COULD', 'LED', 'SISTER', 'BOTH', 'TWO'. Other distinctive forms were also noted e.g., *-ww-* in 'BLOW', 'JAW', etc, *-chch-* in 'STRETCH', etc—all of which have a dialectal distribution in Middle English. See *LALME*, *passim* for data and maps (though for *-ww-* see Smith, *Studies*, Vol II, p.788).

34 Areas outside the test tranches were carefully scanned for forms not occurring there. The purpose of the tranches was to elicit statistically meaningful data for very frequent items. A full account of the tranches is given in Smith, *Studies*, Vol I, pp.17, 193–4.

35 *Pace* Ramsey, 'Palaeography', pp.113–14. See A McIntosh, 'A New Approach to Middle English Dialectology', *English Studies* 44, 1963, 1–11 (repr in *Middle English Dialectology*, chapter 2), esp. note 8 and reference there cited.

36 Ramsey, 'Palaeography', pp.107–9.

37 Ramsey, 'Palaeography', p.133.

38 Viz., the *ȝ/y* contrast, the *wyf, lyf/wijf, lijf* contrast, the *ur/er* contrast, the *na/nought* contrast, the -ø/-*e* contrast. Ramsey's table of contrasts is discussed further below.

39 See A McIntosh, 'Word geography in the lexicography of mediæval English', *Annals of the New York Academy of Sciences* 211, 1973, 55–66 (repr in *Middle English Dialectology*, chapter 7), p.61; also Benskin and Laing, 'Translations and *Mischsprachen*', *passim*.

40 Benskin and Laing, 'Translations and *Mischsprachen*', p.56.

41 Benskin and Laing, 'Translations and *Mischsprachen*'.

42 Benskin and Laing, 'Translations and *Mischsprachen*', p.83.

43 See R W Chambers and M Daunt, *A Book of London English 1384–1425*, OUP: Oxford, 1931. For linguistic profiles of localised and localisable London texts at this time, see *LALME*, Vol III, pp.298–301.

44 See *LALME* Vol IV, *passim*; but for *nough* 'NOT' etc, see Smith, *Studies*, Vol II, p.738.

45 For *drynclyng*, see citations in the *Middle English Dictionary*. The Goettingen MS *Cursor Mundi* occurrence recorded there is now believed to stem from an East Anglian exemplar; I am grateful to Professor Angus McIntosh for this information. For other forms, see *LALME*, *passim*.

46 For the distribution of the forms, see primarily *LALME* Vol I: Dot Maps.

47 See *LALME* Vol. I, p.429. The form *oge* recorded as a minor variable in Worcestershire appears there only in the very early MS Trinity Cambridge, 323; for reservations as to the usefulness of this MS, see *LALME*, Vol III, p.558 (Linguistic Profile 7721).

48 See *LALME*, Vol IV, *passim*; but for *nough* 'NOT' etc see note 44 above and reference there cited.

49 Best indicated in the Dot Maps in *LALME*, Vol I, *passim*. That final *-e* was lost earlier in the North has long been known; see, for instance, R. Jordan, trans. E J Crook, *Handbook of Middle English Grammar: Phonology*, Mouton: The Hague, 1974, pp.141–2.

50 On the principle of minimising numbers of possible layers, see reference cited in note 42 above.

51 See Smith, *Studies*, Vol II, *passim*.

52 See Smith, *Studies*, Vol I, pp.218–19 and references there cited.

53 Doyle and Parkes, 'The production of copies', p.177. For the Taylor Gower, see J J Griffiths, '*Confessio Amantis*: the poem and its pictures', in A J Minnis ed., *Gower's Confessio Amantis: responses and reassessments*, Brewer: Cambridge, 1983, 163–78.

54 Full discussion of these MSS and their individual peculiarities appears in Smith, *Studies*, Vol I chapter 4 (with the exception of the Taylor MS, intensive study of which has only recently become possible for scholars). As indicated there, the probably archetypal language of the Trevisa and Langland traditions is itself South-Western/South-West Midland, but the Western forms of the putative Scribe D are distinguishable from them.

55 See M L Samuels and J J Smith, 'The Language of Gower', *Neuphilologische Mitteilungen* 82, 1981, 295–304 (repr as chapter 3 above).

56 See Smith, *Studies*, Vol I, pp.312–19.

57 See Smith, *Studies*, Vol I, chapter 3 and pp.296–301.

58 Doyle and Parkes, 'The production of copies', p.185.

59 See *LALME*, Vol IV *passim*; for *-ww-*, *e*-prefixes, 'NOT', 'SAW', see Smith, *Studies*, Vol II, pp.778, 735, 738 and 761 respectively.

60 For the analyses, with full citations of main, rarer and sporadic forms see Smith, *Studies*, Vol II.

61 See note 54 above and reference there cited.

62 See *LALME*, Vol IV *passim*.

63 Benskin and Laing, 'Translations and *Mischsprachen*', p.72.

64 See *LALME*, Vol I, p.440.

65 Ramsey, 'Palaeography', p.133.

66 All these differences can be explained in terms of dialectal constraint; see above, pp.56–58.

67 I find Ramsey's defence (Ramsey, 'Palaeography', p.119) of his restricting himself to contrasts unconvincing, for reasons already given by Samuels, 'The Scribe of the Hengwrt and Ellesmere MSS', pp.54–6 (now pp.41–43 above). However, even on his own terms Ramsey's contrasts for Ha4/Cp are misleading; for some— but not all—change quite radically in the course of copying the MSS. Thus Ramsey records, from the *General Prologue* to the *Man of Law's Tale*, a marked preference for *-y-* in Ha4 where Cp has *-i-*, thus;

Tale \ Contrast	Ha4: *y*/Cp: *i*	Ha4: *i*/Cp: *y*
GP	115 occurrences	34
KnT	472	54
MilT	138	20
RvT	69	9
CkT-Gam	163	24
MLT	220	18
	1177	159

Such figures are superficially impressive. However, analysis from later in the MS shows a reversal of this tendency:

Tale \ Contrast	Ha4: *i*/Cp: *y*	Ha4: *y*/Cp: *i*
CanYP+T	90	57
PhysT	13	15
PardP+T	84	27
	187	99

It is possible that Ramsey might suggest that yet further hands are at work in this MS. However, over the same tranche of text, another tendency remains more-or-less the same: the reflexes of OE *ge-* in *I-*/*y-*. In his tranche of text, Ramsey records 77 places where Ha4 has *I-* to Cp's *y-*, and only 2 places where Cp has *I-* to Ha4's *y-*. This tendency remains the same in the tranche I examined for this purpose: 20 places where Ha4 has *I-* to Cp's *y-*, no places at all where Cp has *I-* for *y-*in Ha4. Such opposed tendencies indicate that Ramsey's table has no validity for the interpretations he puts upon it.

I would argue, however, that these figures are essentially beside the point. In the tranche of text I examined, there are 38 places where a reflex of OE *ge-* appears in both MSS. By restricting himself to contrasts, Ramsey would miss the fact that, in 14 places, both MSS have *y-* and, in 4 places, both MSS have *I-*. To use the terminology of constrained variation, both *I-* and *y-* are in the spelling-repertoires of Ha4 and Cp; but something, most probably exemplar-conditioning, has activated *I-* more frequently in Ha4 than Cp.

68 Ramsey, 'Palaeography', p.124.

69 For the relevant analyses, see Smith *Studies*, Vol II, pp.516–42, 554–76.

70 Smith, *Studies*, Vol I, chapter 4, pp.237–8.

71 Manly and Rickert, *Canterbury Tales*, Vol I, pp.221–4.

72 Dean's findings are quoted from Manly and Rickert, *Canterbury Tales*, Vol I, p.222. For Furnivall's account, see F J Furnivall ed., *The Harleian MS 7334 of the Canterbury Tales*, Chaucer Society: London, 1885, p.vi.

73 See citations in *LALME*. Dot maps for *-us* and *-ur* appears in Smith, *Studies*, Vol II, pp.746, 767.

74 Data available in Smith, *Studies*, Vol II, pp.554–76.

75 Smith, *Studies*, Vol I, pp.238–41

76 Manly and Rickert, *Canterbury Tales*, Vol I, p.223.

77 Data available in Smith, *Studies*, Vol II, pp.516–42. It should be noted that Ramsey's massing together of, for instance, *-y-*/*-i-* contrasts across various words thereby disguises a number of interesting shifts in individual words, such as these.

78 See Smith, *Studies*, Vol I, pp.229–31.

79 J J Smith, 'Linguistic features of some fifteenth-century Middle English manuscripts', in D A Pearsall ed., *Manuscripts and Readers in Fifteenth-Century England*, Brewer: Cambridge, 1983, 104–12, p.111.

80 See Smith, *Studies*, chapter 5; also chapter 9 below.

81 D's behaviour contrasts with that of Scribe Δ, whose handwriting is considered by Doyle and Parkes, 'The production of copies', p.206, to be 'remarkably close' to that of scribe D. They detect the hand of scribe Δ in five MSS:

St John's, Cambridge H.1(204) and
BL Addl 24194 (both MSS of Trevisa's translation of Higden's *Polychronicon*);
BL Royal 18.c.xxii (Gower, *Confessio Amantis*);
Brasenose, Oxford 9 (Nicholas Love's *Life of Christ*);
Paris, Bibliothèque nationale, anglais 25 (Guy de Chauliac's *Cyrurgie*).

The language of the MSS copied by Scribe Δ is discussed in Smith, *Studies* Vol I, pp.139–141. Brasenose 9 has been localised to South Buckinghamshire in *LALME*; its linguistic profile appears in Vol III, pp.18–19 (LP6710). It is noticeable that, for 'OWN' (adj.), the usual form in those of Δ's MSS which I have examined (i.e. all but the St John's MS) is *owne*. As far as I can detect, *oghne* appears—and then sporadically—only in the MS of Gower's *Confessio Amantis* where it is, of course, the archetypal form. The distinctive mixture of SW Midland forms and *oughne* in non-Gowerian MSS found in D's MSS is here lacking. This would support the contention of Doyle and Parkes that D and Δ are separate scribes.

7 LANGLAND'S DIALECT

M L Samuels

I

An editor of *Piers Plowman* is not in the same position as editors of Gower or Chaucer. In the case of Gower, the Fairfax and Stafford MSS have now been shown to be as good, dialectally, as a holograph;[1] and in the case of Chaucer, too, we now have strong evidence on which to base reconstructed texts.[2] But, as the doyen of *Piers Plowman* editors, George Kane, has remarked, the dialect of the author of the poem is not recoverable;[3] and if by this we mean that there is no surviving MS that is either holograph or can be proved to be in his language, then that is strictly true. But that does not mean that we have insufficient evidence to define what dialect Langland used, and that will be the main subject of what follows here. Whether the definition would enable us to reconstruct the text is a more difficult question to which we shall return in conclusion.

The definition of Langland's dialect has progressed little in the past century. Skeat, in the terminology of dialect definition typical of his age, stated that it is 'mainly Midland with occasional introduction of Southern forms', adding later in the same section that it belonged to the west rather than to the east of England.[4] R W Chambers, who was mainly concerned with the problem of authorship, emphasised the 'provincialism' of certain forms.[5] J P Oakden thought that a fresh investigation would achieve little to the purpose, because 'at best it would only be possible to localise the dialect of the various manuscripts', not the original dialect.[6] R Kaiser referred to 'Unsicherheit um die Herkunft des *Piers Plowman*',[7] and, finally and most recently in their monumental edition of the B-Text, George Kane and E T Donaldson remark in a footnote:

> We are aware that Langland's native dialect is unlikely to have been that of [MS] W. But then there is no evidence that he wrote *Piers Plowman* in that native dialect, any more than that he retained this in adulthood.[8]

This is an admirably reasonable disclaimer from editors who know better than to work from anything but sound and proven premises. What follows here is not intended as a criticism of their views, but is offered simply as an attempt to extend our knowledge in a field which seems hitherto to have been insufficiently explored.

The types of evidence normally available for establishing the dialect of a ME author are as follows:

1 forms determined by rhyme and alliteration;
2 where there is a textual tradition of some homogeneity, the evidence of the texts themselves, especially of forms that can be shown to belong to a previous layer of copying and are therefore *relict* and potentially archetypal or authorial;
3 internal autobiographical evidence;
4 external biographical evidence;
5 the dialectal distribution of the surviving texts, showing the areas of regional circulation of the work.

The evidence of 3 and 4 is that Langland was born in SE Shropshire, spent at least part of his youth in the Malvern area[9] and later lived in London, but it is evidence that has hitherto lacked corroboration from 1, 2 or 5. Of these three, 2 has proved the greatest obstacle: the A- and B-MSS were subject to so many different forms of copying in different dialects that it has been found difficult to distinguish the different copyists' layers. However, with our increased knowledge of ME dialect differentiations,[10] a new attempt may prove worthwhile. But in order to make that attempt, the evidence of 1 and 5 is relevant and will be considered first.

II

In the controversy over multiple versus single authorship, part of the evidence adduced was to the effect that the alliterative practices were, on the one hand, idiosyncratic, and, on the other, consistent throughout all three versions. As Donaldson put it in 1949, 'in alliteration the three versions of *Piers Plowman* resemble closely nothing but each other'.[11] In the Kane-Donaldson edition of the B-Text, the characterisation of Langland's alliterative system as 'ingeniously expeditious' implies that it was arbitrarily selected from a wide range of possible choices to suit his purposes, rather than the natural result of his own dialectal system.[12] It is true that in his earlier work Donaldson seriously considered the possiblity that the *f/v*-alliteration was dialectally conditioned, but this was raised mainly as a point in favour of single authorship, since it was so unlikely that all the four separate poets of the multiple authorship theory could have 'formed a little colony of f-voicing poets resident in London'.[13] The Kane-Donaldson edition, however, allows no more than that *f/v*-alliteration *may* have been an exact rhyme in Langland's dialect.[14]

More recently, Professor Kane has repeated his assessment of Langland's choice of certain dialect forms as due to 'alliterative convenience', but reappraises it as 'eclecticism instancing the same independence and originality which characterises the style and content of his poem'.[15] However, his argument, which demonstrates Langland's control of the alliterative medium, is by no means dependent on the assumption of this particular eclecticism; on the contrary, his case for Langland's excellence would be considerably enhanced, not weakened, if the assumption of 'alliterative convenience' were shown to be unnecessary.

Now, what constitutes the basis of a set of alliterative practices is a question that evidently requires further consideration. That it involves some degree of stylistic choice is not in dispute; what now appears to be in need of emphasis is that that choice will normally be based on the poet's own linguistic system. Since conventional end-rhyme provides an exact parallel, it will serve as an illustration. Suppose we were studying the text of a ME poet who used end-rhyme, not alliteration, as his medium, but we found that his rhymes were idiosyncratic. The first and most natural explanation we would turn to would be his dialect system; only after that, if there still remained rhymes that disagreed with the most likely dialect system, would we admit that the poet might have borrowed a rhyme from another system. Then, if the borrowed rhyme succeeded in contributing some special effect, it would qualify as a merit, but if it was used purely *metri gratia* we would think rather less of the poet. In other words, we normally assume, as a sound critical canon, that poetic practices are founded on a natural and consistent linguistic system, and that any additions or mixtures must have special justification (as, for example, in the case of Spenser).

The same argument, surely, must apply to alliterative poets. As is well known, certain details of Langland's alliterative practice were borrowed from his northern precursors to give special effect; but we have no right to assume that the remainder was anything else but part of his normal dialect, i.e. the natural result of applying the basic principle of alliteration to his own language.

There are, therefore, strong *a priori* grounds for believing that a ME poet's alliterative practices are based on his dialect; indeed, on the analogy of end-rhyme one could go further and say that the onus of proof lies with those who deny the connection. However, it is not proposed here to argue any further the theoretical probabilities of this question. Instead, let us suppose, initially for the sake of argument only, that Langland's alliterative practices *were* based on his dialect and see what result that produces.

It is essential first to recognise that lexis, the open system of language, can be easily altered or added to, whereas the closed systems of phonology and grammar are far more basic and less likely to be altered. The Northern or North Midland *k*-and *g*-alliterations (as in *kirke*, *give*, *gar* 'cause') are really no more than individual instances of lexical adaptation, and must be set aside as a feature in which Langland was to some small degree conforming to the tradition of his medium. For our present purpose, only genuinely grammatical and phonological criteria are to be considered, the most important of which are the following four:

(i) For the word 'she', the alliteration demands the form *heo* (less probably *he*)[16] more frequently than the form *sche* or *scheo*. This restricts the area of provenance to the Western and Southern dialects, apart from east Essex and south-east Suffolk (see Fig. 1), and it excludes London.

(ii) 'Are' is alliterated on *ar(e)n* as well as on forms in *b*-(*beþ*, *beoþ*, *buþ*, *ben*). This excludes the Southern dialects and restricts the fairly large area indicated in (i) to the West Midlands only. In this area *ar(e)n* was used in varying degrees of frequency, but usually as a minority variant to the *b*-forms. For the xiv century, this criterion would also exclude Gloucestershire (see line B on Fig. 2).[17]

(iii) *Piers Plowman* and *Mum and the Sothsegger* are the only two works to show consistent *f*/*v*-alliteration,[18] and this is strong evidence that they are both from the Southern area showing voicing of *f* to *v*.[19] When combined with (i) and (ii) above, this criterion limits the provenance of *Piers Plowman* to Herefordshire and south-west Worcestershire (see line A on Fig. 2).

(iv) Alliteration of *h*- with initial vowels is prominent in two works from different areas, *Piers Plowman* and *Sir Gawain*.[20] The phonetic basis for this usage existed in dialects which—on the evidence of those texts that show dialect features most closely—either add an unetymological *h*- (as in south-Worcestershire *hart* 'art') or omit etymological *h*- (as in Gloucestershire *ast* 'hast'). The different areas where this could occur in Middle English are capable of precise delimitation: for the area here in question it is limited to a patch running from Warwickshire through south Worcestershire to Gloucestershire (see line C on Fig. 2), and thus excludes Herefordshire.[21]

We are thus left with SW Worcestershire as the only area where the above four features could co-occur. The only other area that might be considered is the

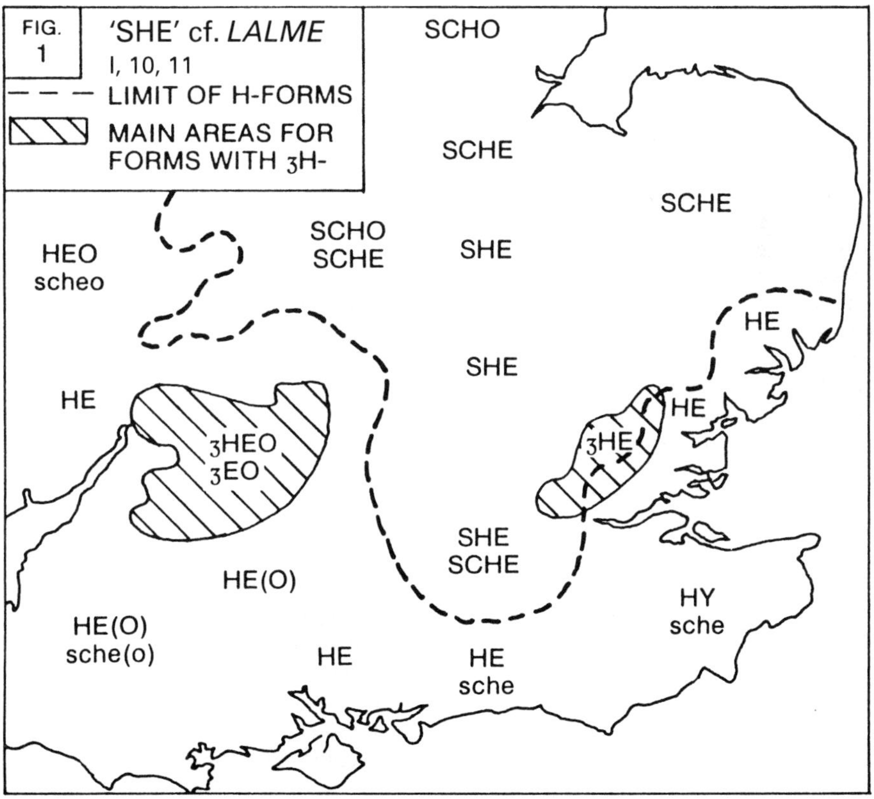

FIG. 2

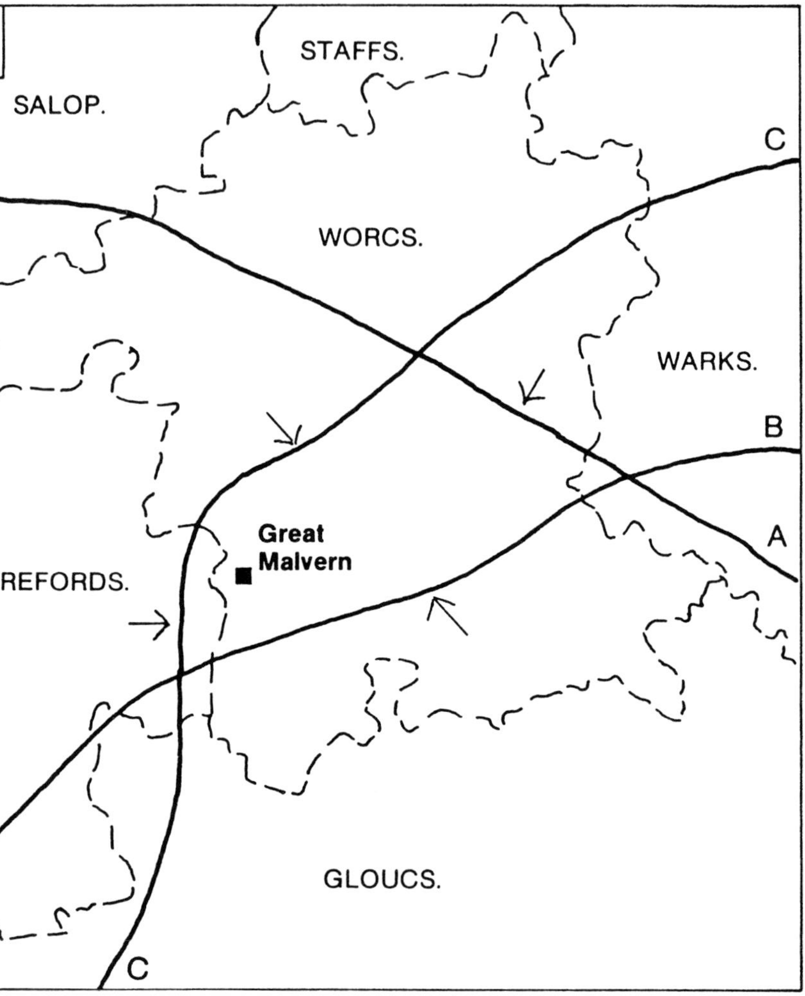

eastern coastal strip referred to in (i) above; but, as we shall see later, the relict forms in the MS traditions are invariably Western, not Eastern. It is therefore possible to state that Langland's dialect, as evidenced by his alliterative practice, *can be assigned to SW Worcestershire and nowhere else*.

The fact that this tallies exactly with the Malvern of the internal evidence can hardly be pure coincidence. Such a remarkable correspondence must surely entitle us to conclude that Langland's unusual alliterative practices are confirmed as dialectally conditioned, and, conversely, that Malvern is confirmed as the place of both his upbringing and his dialect.

However, it is not simply for such corroboration that the alliterative evidence is important. It also has special significance for the question under discussion: whether Langland was, or was not, a dialect speaker in his adult life. As is well known, changes in linguistic habits are unusual after the age of twenty-five. Certainly lexical usage can alter at any time, for that need involve no more than the simplest code-switching; but there is not likely to be much change in accent or grammar, and none in phonemic system. We know from strong internal evidence that Langland was at least thirty when he wrote the A-version,[22] yet his choice of alliterative practices, as shown by grammatical and phonological criteria, was quite evidently dialectal, and it continued unchanged throughout the B- and C-versions. This is a strong indication that his dialect remained basically that of Malvern throughout; the fact that he used lexis suitable for a London audience and excluded specifically Western words is really a separate matter.[23]

But the real question to be answered here is how Langland would have spelt. The position in Middle English, with its widespread traditions of local spelling, was very different from that of today. People learned the dialect spelling of the place in which they were brought up, and could never, thereafter, wholly succeed in wiping their dialect-spelling slates clean in order to learn a new system.[24] The best-known examples of change are those who had an interest in changing—professional scribes and, in the fifteenth century, those connected with government.[25] Clerical writers, on the other hand, were less likely to change, or, if they did, the result is no more than a transparent mixture of their own dialect forms with others that they deemed to be more prestigious.[26] Then, if we are thinking of Langland as a poet rather than a cleric, there is the parallel of Gower, who can now be proved to have retained the regional spellings of his youth.[27] Finally, there is also the difference in period to be borne in mind; in the fifteenth century there was a prestige form of the language at which writers could aim, whereas in the fourteenth century there was not.

On balance, therefore, it seems unlikely that Langland would have changed from the spelling he had learned in his youth. But for corroboration of this view we must now turn to the texts.

III

The A-texts can tell us little about the provenance of their archetype or the dialect in which it was written. They demonstrate a situation that is found elsewhere in the history of textual criticism, in which the oldest MSS of a work (or their descendants) are found on the periphery of the culture.[28] Eleven of them are in the language of their copyists, or of antecedent copyists, as follows (in this and subsequent lists the predominant dialect—normally that of the uppermost layer—is specified , but there are usually varying amounts of relict forms from previous copyings):

A Bodl Ashmole 1468: west Norfolk.[29]
E Trinity Coll, Dublin D.4.12: Durham or Northumberland.[30]
H BL Harley 875: north-west Warwickshire.[31]
H_3 BL Harley 3954: south Norfolk.[32]
J Pierpont Morgan Libr NY, M818 (*olim* Ingilby): Lincolnshire.[33]
L London, Lincoln's Inn, MS 150: south-west Shropshire.[34]

- M London, Society of Antiquaries, MS 687: north-west Suffolk.[35]
- R Bodl Rawlinson poet. 137: south-west Sussex.[36]
- U University Coll, Oxford 45: south Cambridgeshire.[37]
- V Bodl Eng. Poet. a.1 (*olim* Vernon): north Worcestershire.[38]

MS U, while predominantly in the language of its copyist, also shows some Northern forms. This phenomenon is common in London MSS of ca.1400 and seems to have arisen because northern scribes working in London tended to copy very literally and exactly with just the occasional lapse into their own spelling. Such sprinklings of Northern forms are thus a useful indication of London origin, even though the dialect of the later copyist was not London. They recur frequently in the B-texts and in Chaucer MSS.

The remainder of the A-texts are in mixed dialects which usually show two strata, one Eastern and the other Western. However, the strata lack any more specific dialect colouring and are therefore difficult to localise. In two of these, T (Cambridge, Trinity Coll MS R.3.14) and N (Aberystwyth, NL of Wales, MS 733B), the Western forms appear to be relict and therefore belong to the earlier stratum, but they are not specific enough dialectally to provide any clues. T does, however, contain a few forms which, if considered in the light of certain B- and C-MSS to be discussed below, might qualify as authorial.[39] On the other hand MSS H and V, though themselves in W Midland dialects, cannot be proved to be formally any nearer to the archetype than the rest and might indeed, for all we know, be re-translations into their Worcestershire and Warwickshire dialects from London exemplars. It is noteworthy that in V the text of *Piers Plowman* is less fully W Midland than the other texts in this collection, some of its forms suggesting that it was derived from an eastern exemplar.[40]

The C-text MSS are in strong contrast to those of the A-text. With two exceptions they form a dialectally cohesive SW Midland group, as follows:

- D Bodl Douce 104: Hiberno-English.[41]
- E Bodl Laud Misc 656: N Oxfordshire.[42]
- F CUL Ff.v.35: mid-Oxfordshire.[43]
- G CUL Dd.iii.13: SE Herefordshire and NW Gloucestershire borders.[44]
- I University Libr, London V.88. (*olim* Ilchester): copied in London from a SW Worcestershire exemplar.[45]
- K Bodl Digby 171: SE Herefordshire.[46]
- M BL Cotton Vespasian B.XVI: W Warwickshire.[47]
- N BL Harley 2376: SE Herefordshire.[48]
- P Huntington, Cal., HM 137 (*olim* Phillipps 8231): Gloucestershire - Monmouthshire border.[49]
- P_2 BL Addl 34779 (*olim* Phillipps 9056): SE Shropshire.[50]
- Q CUL Addl 4325: NW Gloucestershire.[51]
- S Corpus Christi, Cambridge 293: S Herefordshire.[52]
- St University Libr, London Sterling V.17 (*olim* Clopton): W Worcestershire.[53]
- U BL Addl 35157: copied by a NW Worcestershire scribe from a SW Worcestershire exemplar.[54]

V Trinity Coll Dublin, D.4.1 (212) NW Gloucestershire.[55]
X Huntington, Cal., HM 143: SW Worcestershire, but with some slight signs of interference typical of a London copying.[56]
Y Bodl Digby 102: SW Worcestershire.

It seems likely that a majority of the C-MSS (or their immediate antecedents) were written locally in the SW Midland areas indicated by their dialects, and not by immigrant scribes in London. One indication of this is furnished by a comparison with the B-MSS written in London: as will appear below, these show great variety of scribal dialects and layers, and it would therefore be very strange indeed if each C-MS (if written in London) had found a SW Midland scribe. Secondly, the actual distribution of the dialects of the C-MSS in the SW Midlands may well be significant, for those of the 'better' *i*-group (X, U, Y, I) occupy a central position in the Malvern area, with only D and P_2 as more distant members of the group, whereas the inferior *p*-group seems to have radiated outwards from there to SE Herefordshire, N Gloucestershire, E Warwickshire and N Oxfordshire.[57] That such a distribution could have been the work of a colony of western immigrant scribes in London seems unlikely in the extreme. Finally, the C-MSS show far less evidence of contamination from other dialect copyings than the A- or B-MSS: with the exception of MSS I and X, when any mixture does appear it is, significantly, of local origin, as in U. It is therefore very unlikely that the C-MSS, whether separately or through their archetype, could have been translated back from a London exemplar. If that had been the case, at least a few London relicts would have been expected, but there are none. A very strong pointer to this is the presence or absence of the London relict form *therwhyle(s)* (conj.) 'while', which occurs in no fewer than nine B-MSS (BoCCotHmLMORY), whereas the only C-MS to show it is I, and there it happens to be a well-known distinguishing feature of the latest copyist.[58]

Such a concentration of C-MSS in dialects of the SW Midlands is unlikely to have come about without an authorial presence in the area, and Skeat's view that the author returned to Malvern in later life is thus shown to be highly probable.[59] However, what will be argued below by no means depends on that hypothesis. Whatever the reason for the concentration, the dialectal provenance of the C-MSS supports the conclusions reached in II above regarding Langland's own dialect, and even on the evidence of this correspondence alone it would be reasonable to postulate that his dialect was an antecedent form of those found in the SW Worcestershire C-MSS X, U, Y and I. But since, at this stage of the argument, it could be objected that the dialect of these MSS is due simply to the scribe who copied their archetype and not to Langland himself, we must now turn to the last essential and conclusive link in the evidence, the B-MSS.

As a potential source of original dialect forms, the B-MSS are, in general, unpromising. It is *a priori* likely that a majority of them were written in London, and as already pointed out above with reference to the A-MSS, in London of ca.1400 copying and recopying by scribes of different dialects could result in accumulations of strata that are difficult to disentangle.[60] Three B-MSS, Bm (London, BL Addl 10574), Cot (London, BL Cotton Caligula A.XI) and Bo (Oxford, Bodl Libr Bodley 814) appear to derive certain of their dialectal features from a north Gloucestershire exemplar,[61] itself presumably an intermediate copy in the chain of descent from the B-archetype; in another case, M (London BL Addl 35287), the predominant features suggest a Herefordshire exemplar of similar status.[62] In six other MSS, most earlier dialect features have been eliminated by translation processes (only two are in London language, but some or all of the remainder may well have been copied in London by immigrant scribes):

C_2 CUL Ll.iv.14: Cambridgeshire.[63]
F Corpus Christi, Oxford 201: Essex.[64]
Ht Huntington, Cal., HM 114 (*olim* Phillipps 8252): S Essex.[65]
O Oriel, Oxford 79: N Hertfordshire.[66]
W Trinity, Cambridge B.15.17: London.[67]
Y Newnham, Cambridge (*olim* Yates Thompson): probably London, with diluted Western forms.

There remain, however, two B-MSS of great relevance for our purpose: R (Bodl Rawlinson Poet. 38) and L (Bodl Laud Misc 581). R contains a sprinkling of Northern forms from an intermediate London copying of the type described on p. 76 above, and its uppermost layer was contributed by an immigrant Suffolk scribe;[68] but its main and oldest layer is unmistakably *the same SW Worcestershire dialect as is found in MSS X, U and I of the C-Text*. The particular combination of dialect features that determines this identification is as follows.[69]

1 the spelling *oe* for ME ō, as in *goed* 'good', *noet* 'knows not';
2 *heo* 'she' and *a* for either 'he' or 'she';
3 *noyther* 'neither' and *no* 'nor';
4 *ar* (conj.) 'ere, before';
5 *ȝut* 'yet';
6 *u* and *uy* for OE ȳ̆, as in *huyre* 'hire', *pruyde* 'pride'.

The same combination is found in a fainter and more diluted form in L. There can be little doubt that it is archetypal, for, although L and R are not especially closely linked by substantive textual agreements,[70] they often correspond in their distributions of variant forms, e.g., of *any* and *eny*, *ȝif* and *if*, *com(e)* and *cam* 'came', *byȝunde* and *byȝende* 'beyond'.[71] Since it is very unlikely that such non-substantive variation could be due to contamination, it must be presumed to be archetypal.

When this original layer in the B-MSS is identified with the language of the C-MSS X, Y and I, the only point of discrepancy that arises is the forms for 'she'. Here, the older Western form *heo* is preserved only in the B-MSS, whereas X has *he*, Y has the more modern *she*, and I has the slightly more southerly *ȝhe*, a later variant of the *ȝheo* in Fig. 1. As will be shown in IV below, it is much more likely that the C-archetype had *heo* beside *sche(o)*.

It is thus possible to establish that the archetypal dialect of both the B- and the C-texts was the identical dialect of SW Worcestershire, and it is this correspondence between two independent traditions that provides us with the link essential for our conclusion: that the dialect of SW Worcestershire, already pinpointed for us by Langland's alliterative practices, was in fact the one that he used in his holographs. The evidence of the A-MSS is not against this: it is not at all surprising that in that tradition, apart from some relicts in T,[72] the specific identifying features did not survive the repeated processes of copying and translation.

What is here postulated, then, is that the SW Worcestershire stratum in the B-MSS L and R is Langland's own. One can, of course, always invent some SW Worcestershire scribe of straw who was providentially at Langland's elbow in those two widely separated periods when the B- and C-versions were committed from holograph to archetype; but that, surely, must remain the less probable alternative.

IV

To return now to the question posed earlier: is it possible to reconstruct Langland's dialect? According to the conclusion reached above, the MSS that are likely to be nearest to it are those whose language can be located in the Malvern area, in particular the C-MS X, but with reference where necessary to the C-MSS I, U and Y. Since, as mentioned above, these MSS may well show some modernisations or other scribal changes, the status of their language must be determined by comparing it with other ME evidence from S Worcestershire, which consists of the following:

1 MS Phillipps 12086, a miscellany written at Worcester ca.1450.[73]
2 Bodl Rawlinson C.81, a volume of medical works written at Pershore (Worcestershire), early fifteenth century.[74]
3 Bodl Digby 86, a late-thirteenth-century collection of French and English verse, with marginals connecting it with Ridmerley (SW Worcestershire), a location confirmed by its language.[75]
4 Bodl Rawlinson D.100 (*Mandeville's Travels*), early fifteenth century.[76]
5 Bodl Laud Misc. 463 (*Southern Legendary*), ca.1400.
6 Trinity, Cambridge B.14.39 (323), a late-thirteenth-century miscellany.
7 Huntington Cal., HM 125 (*Prick of Conscience*), early fifteenth century.
8 Worcester, Chapter Libr F.10 (sermons), ca.1400.

Of these, texts 1–4 contain non-linguistic evidence of localisation, and on the basis of their linguistic features texts 5–8 may be assigned with certainty to the same area. The most important diagnostic feature for S Worcestershire texts is *oe* for ME $\bar{o}$, as in *goed* 'good' (it also appears in certain Gloucestershire texts, but these are easily distinguished on other grounds). That it was no mere transient fashion is shown by the fact that it occurs in six of the eight texts (Nos. 2–7) over the whole time-span. In addition, the *ae*-spelling (as in *maed* 'made'), which is extremely rare in Middle English, occurs in No. 5; the unmarked pronominal form *a* ('he' or 'she') occurs in Nos. 6 and 8, *noyþer* 'neither' in Nos. 7 and 8, and *ar* (conj.) 'before' in Nos. 3, 5, 6, 7 and 8. Of all the identifying features listed in III above, only *ȝut* 'yet' finds no parallel in this group of S Worcestershire texts, and this is easily accounted for by the fact that the *Piers Plowman* texts, if located at Malvern, are the most westerly of the group and have this feature in common with Herefordshire and Gloucestershire texts to the west and south.

The evidence of these texts shows that Langland's alliteration on *heo* as well as *sche* is entirely in agreement with the dialect of the area. Texts, 1, 2, 7 and 8 all have *s(c)he*, texts 3 and 4 *hoe*, 5 has *she*, *heo* and *sheo*, and 6 has *ho*, *hoe*, *heo*, *he* and *hue*. Langland was simply availing himself of two of the variants that existed in his own dialect, and not, as Chambers thought, combining his own provincial *heo* with a *she-* form that he learned in London.[77] This evidence also confirms that he is more likely to have used *heo*, as attested by the relict stratum in the B-MSS, than the *he* that is found in X.[78]

In most other respects, however, and apart from certain errors and Northern forms induced in the course of transmission, MS X probably provides a fair representation of Langland's dialect. The typically W Midland rounding before nasals as in *mony*, *mon*, *con* was recessive in Worcestershire, so that when we find *mony* varying with *many*, but *man* and *can*, that is a distribution paralleled in other texts (e.g., No. 7). The other typical Westernism, rounded vowels descending from OE y̆̄, usually survives except before nasals, as in *fuyr* 'fire', *pruyde* 'pride', *buggen* 'buy', compared with *synne* 'sin', *kynde* 'nature'; and this distribution, too, occurs elsewhere in Worcestershire (e.g., in text No. 4). There are even numerous variables that can be regarded as part of the same Worcestershire dialect, and are not necessarily due to textual mixture: e.g., *ech* and *vch* 'each', *suluen* and *siluen* 'self', *suluer* and *seluer* 'silver', *beth*, *buth*, *ben* and *aren* 'are'. The same applies to variations in the endings *-ur* and *-ir*, *-us* and *-is*, *-ud* and *-id*.

A more difficult problem is posed by final *-e*, for here the evidence of texts from the same area is no certain guide. As I have suggested elsewhere,[79] in the late fourteenth century in S England the use of *-e* depended on varying conditions of stress and register, and the individual usage of an author cannot be established simply on the evidence of when and where he lived. If there is no holograph, the only other possible evidence is the author's practice in writing syllabic metre. The conclusions that can be drawn from stressed metre are much less certain. One possible indication is from half-lines that would, without *-e*, be too short to fall into any of the recognised stress patterns. For example, at B.IX.19, MS L (Skeat's text) reads 'bi his first wyf,' which lacks the weak adjective *-e* after *first* and the dative *-e* after *wyf*. The Kane-Donaldson reading 'bi his firste wyue' is that of their base-text, W, and that is borne out by the reading of X, 'by his furste wyue'. This and other similar cases show that Langland must have made at least some use of grammatical final *-e*. In MS X, the *-e* is to some extent over-represented, and Kane and Donaldson's MS W may well give a fairer representation of it, even though the language of that MS is London, not Worcestershire. In any case, it is perfectly reasonable to read the B-text in the form in which it would have been best understood by the London audience for which it was intended.

The conclusions reached above may be summarised as follows:

1 Langland's alliterative practice provides very strong evidence that his dialect was that of SW Worcestershire, which is then found to tally with the Malvern area of internal evidence.
2 The C-MSS X, I and Y are, in basis, in SW Worcestershire dialect, and the evidence of 1 above at least suggests that that basis is authorial. But the deciding factor is the close correspondence between it and the relict stratum in the B-MSS L and R. This greatly increases the probability that the features of that stratum, together with many more in the C-MSS, are authorial.
3 The reconstruction of Langland's dialect could probably be best achieved by adopting X as the basis and modifying it in a conservative direction.[80]

NOTES

1 M L Samuels and J J Smith, 'The language of Gower', *Neuphilologische Mitteilungen* 82, 1981, 295–304 (repr as chapter 3 above).
2 M L Samuels, 'Chaucer's spelling', in D Gray and E G Stanley eds, *Middle English Studies presented to Norman Davis*, OUP: Oxford, 1983, 17–37 (repr as chapter 4 above).
3 G Kane, *Piers Plowman: the Evidence for Authorship*, Athlone: London, 1965, pp.3, 10.
4 W W Skeat ed., *The Vision of William concerning Piers the Plowman, in three parallel texts*, OUP: Oxford, 1886, II, pp.lvii-lviii.
5 R W Chambers, 'The three texts of *Piers Plowman* and their grammatical forms', *Modern Language Review* 14, 1919, 149–51.
6 J P Oakden, *Alliterative Poetry in Middle English: the Dialectal and Metrical Survey*, MUP: Manchester, 1930, p.61.
7 R Kaiser, *Zur Geographie des mittelenglischen Wortschatzes*, Palaestra 205: Leipzig, 1937, p.317.
8 G Kane and E T Donaldson eds, *Piers Plowman: the B Version*, Athlone: London, 1975, p.215, note 181.
9 Skeat, *The Vision of William*, II, p.xxxi; D Pearsall ed., *Piers Plowman: an edition of the C-Text*, Arnold: London, 1978, p.28 and references there quoted.
10 See A McIntosh, 'A new approach to Middle English dialectology', *English Studies* 44, 1963, 1–11 (now repr in *Middle English Dialectology*, chapter 2); M Benskin, 'Local archives and Middle English dialects', *Journal of the Society of Archivists* 5, 1977, 500–14; also *LALME*.
11 E T Donaldson, *Piers Plowman: the C-Text and its Poet*, Yale UP: New Haven, 1949, p.43.
12 Kane and Donaldson, *Piers Plowman B*, p.132.
13 Donaldson, *The C-Text*, p.46.
14 Kane and Donaldson, *Piers Plowman B*, p.133.
15 G Kane, 'Music "neither unpleasant nor monotonous"', in P L Heyworth ed., *Mediæval Studies for J A W Bennett*, OUP: Oxford, 1981, pp.43–4.
16 Cf. Fig.1: although *he* was a common Southern and Western variant, the fact that the non-Eastern form *heo* often survives as a relict in Eastern A- and B-MSS shows that it is to be preferred.
17 Cf. *LALME* I, maps 118–20.

18 Donaldson, *The C-Text*, p.44; S S Hussey, 'Langland's reading of alliterative poetry', *Modern Language Review* 60, 1965, 163–170.
19 Cf. *LALME* I, map 1180.
20 Oakden, *Alliterative Poetry*, p.162.
21 Cf. *LALME* I, maps 1172–3.
22 S S Hussey ed., *Piers Plowman: Critical Approaches*, Methuen: London, 1969, p.10; J A W Bennett, 'The date of the A-text of *Piers Plowman*', *Publications of the Modern Language Association of America* 58, 1943, 566–72. I accept here the standard arguments for the dating of the A- and B-texts on the principle that, if knowledge of certain well-recorded events is shown, it is irrelevant whether that knowledge belongs to Langland himself or to his Dreamer. But even the minimum age of thirty that I postulate for Langland can be deduced without risk of what Professor Kane, in his Chambers Memorial Lecture of 1965, called the 'autobiographical fallacy', for it is very unlikely that Langland would have attempted to describe the religious, moral and emotional conflicts of someone else of 45 years old if he himself was younger than that at the time of the B-revision.
23 The rarity of specifically W Midland words in *Piers Plowman* is noted by R W V Elliott, 'The Langland country', in Hussey, *Critical Approaches*, 226–44, p.242.
24 M Benskin and M Laing, 'Translations and *Mischsprachen* in Middle English Manuscripts', in M Benskin and M L Samuels eds, *So Meny People Longages and Tonges: Philological Essays in Scots and Mediaeval English presented to Angus McIntosh*, MEDP: Edinburgh, 1981, 55–106; and cf. *LALME* Vol I, pp. 12–23.
25 N Davis, 'A scribal problem in the Paston Letters', *English and Germanic Studies* 4, 1951–2, 31–64; N Davis, 'A Paston Hand', *Review of English Studies*, new series 3, 1952, 209–21; M L Samuels, 'Spelling and dialect in the late and post-Middle English periods', in Benskin and Samuels, *So Meny People*, 43–54 (repr as chapter 8 below); A I Doyle, 'University College, Oxford, MS 97 and its relationship to the Simeon Manuscript (BL Addl 22283)', in Benskin and Samuels, *So Meny People*, 265–82; M L Samuels, 'The scribe of the Hengwrt and Ellesmere Manuscripts of *The Canterbury Tales*', *Studies in the Age of Chaucer* 5, 1983, 49–65 (repr as chapter 5 above); J J Smith, 'Linguistic features of some fifteenth-century Middle English manuscripts', in D Pearsall ed., *Manuscripts and Readers in Fifteenth-Century England*, Brewer: Cambridge, 1983, 104–12, p.111. See also chapter 6 above.
26 A typical example of such a mixture is to be seen in Hand D of Bodl e Musaeo 35, fols. 438–52.
27 Samuels and Smith, 'The language of Gower'.
28 L D Reynolds and N G Wilson, *Scribes and Scholars: a Guide to the Transmission of Greek and Latin Literature*, 2nd edn, OUP: Oxford, 1974, p.248.
29 Forms specific for this localisation are: *sweche* 'SUCH', *aȝenys* 'AGAINST', *henys* 'HENCE', *wer(l)d* 'WORLD', *fryst, frist* 'FIRST', *owyn* 'OWN', *fere* 'FIRE', *wol* 'WELL' (adv.), *þorow* 'THROUGH'.
30 Specific forms: *syke* 'SUCH', *mony* 'MANY', *gude* 'GOOD', *er* 'ARE', *þof* 'THOUGH'.
31 Specific forms: *heo* 'SHE', *whuche* 'WHICH', *uche/liche* 'EACH', *mon* (*man*) 'MAN', *ony* 'ANY', *aftur* 'AFTER', *þen* 'THEN', *silf* (*sylue, seluen*) 'SELF'.
32 Specific forms: *hee* 'THEY', *heem, heere* 'THEM', 'THEIR', *aȝyn* 'AGAIN', *er* 'OR', *ho* 'HOW', *fryst* 'FIRST', *wer(l)d* 'WORLD', *myth* 'MIGHT', *xal* 'SHALL', *yorw/thur/your* 'THROUGH', *-ynt* = infinitive + 'IT'.
33 For the language of this MS, see Margaret Laing, *Studies in the dialect material of mediæval Lincolnshire* (Diss. PhD, Edinburgh, 1978), I, 378; II, 148–50.

34 Specific forms: *þeo* 'THE', *(sc)heo* 'SHE', *heo* 'THEY', *mon* 'MAN', *no* (*neo, ny*) 'NOR', *þauȝ(h)/þouȝ* 'THOUGH', *þoruȝ* 'THROUGH', *streynþe* 'STRENGTH', *ey(ȝ)nen* 'EYES', *fache* 'FETCH', *syȝ(h)* 'SAW', *fuf* 'FIVE', *heir* 'HERE'.
35 Specific forms: *wor(l)d* 'WORLD', *myth* 'MIGHT', *iche* 'EACH', *whou* 'HOW', *quan/qwan* 'WHEN', *nout(h)* 'NOT', *scherche* 'CHURCH', *boþen*, *-yn* 'BOTH', *hasked* 'ASKED', *þourth* 'THROUGH'.
36 Specific forms: *hure* 'HEAR', *wordle* 'WORLD', *goud* 'GOOD', *thaþ* 'THAT', *houndred* 'HUNDRED', *many* (*meny*) 'MANY', *ȝut* 'YET', *von-* 'UN-' (prefix), *þorw/þurȝ* 'THROUGH'.
37 Specific forms: *ony* 'ANY', *siche/swich(e)* 'SUCH', *mochil* 'MUCH', *yuel* 'EVIL', *wol* (adv.) 'WELL', *hyngen* (pret.) 'HANGED', *throschfold* 'THRESHOLD'.
38 Specific forms: *whon* 'WHEN', *þauh* 'THOUGH', *serwe* 'SORROW', *oune* 'OWN', *stude* 'STEAD', *hedde* 'HAD', *heo* 'SHE' and 'THEY'. This MS agrees, for a majority of its dialect features, with BL Addl 37787, commonplace book of John Northwood of Bordesley (north-east Worcestershire), ca.1400.
39 The dialect of T is predominantly Eastern, as shown by forms like *woord* 'WORD', *ȝa* 'YES', *blisse* 'BLESS', *henis* 'HENCE', *-ande* pres.part.. However, in addition to the more commonplace Western relicts like *fuyr*, *brugges*, *luþere*, it preserves frequent *heo* 'SHE' as well as occasional *hy* 'THEY' and *a* 'HE'.
40 Thus in *Piers Plowman* V shows *þis* 'THESE', *er* (conj.) 'BEFORE', *after* and *þoruȝ* 'THROUGH', instead of the normal forms *þeos(e)*, *ar/or*, *aftur* and *þorw(h)*, and the former are closer to those of T (*þise*, *er*, *aftir*, *þoruȝ*).
41 Specific forms: *euch* 'EACH', *þai*, *ham*, *har* 'THEY, THEM, THEIR', *silf* 'SELF', *leyngþ* 'LENGTH', *brant* 'BURNT', *hyre* 'HEAR', *stide* 'STEAD', *sig* 'SAY', *ȝewe* 'GIVE', *woch* 'WHICH', *proȝth* 'THROUGH', *þoȝth(þeȝth)* 'THOUGH'. Cf. A McIntosh and M L Samuels, 'Prolegomena to a study of mediaeval Anglo-Irish', *Medium Ævum* 37, 1968, 1–11.
42 Specific forms: *hure* 'HEAR', *ȝo* 'SHE', *myche* 'MUCH', *silf* 'SELF', *þuder* 'THITHER', *to gadres* 'TOGETHER', *forȝutte* 'FORGET', *laste* 'LEST'.
43 Specific forms: *beþynne*, *biþoute* 'WITHIN, WITHOUT', *aftur* 'AFTER', *-us* (plural of nouns), *wurche* (vb.) 'WORK', *wurkes* (sb.) 'WORKS'.
44 Specific forms: *hyre/huyre/here* 'HEAR', *hy* 'THEY', *fram* 'FROM', *gunneþ* (pl. pres.) 'BEGIN', *wordle* 'WORLD', *meny* 'MANY'.
45 On the scribe of this MS, see A I Doyle and M B Parkes, 'The production of copies of the *Canterbury Tales* and the *Confessio Amantis* in the early fifteenth century', in M B Parkes and A G Watson eds, *Mediæval Scribes, Manuscripts and Libraries: Essays presented to N R Ker*, Scolar Press: London, 1978, 163–210; cf. Smith 'Linguistic features'; also J J Smith, *Studies in the language of some manuscripts of Gower's Confessio Amantis* (Diss. PhD, Glasgow, 1985). See also chapter 6 above and chapter 9 below. For specific dialect forms of this MS, see p.78 above.
46 Specific forms: *hure*, *huiren* 'HEAR', *fram* 'FROM', *ny* 'NOR', *ȝut* 'YET', *eolde* 'AGE', *fuld* 'FELLED', *meny/mony* 'MANY'.
47 Specific forms: *here* 'HEAR', *hure*, *heore* 'HER', *swich(e)* 'SUCH', *fur*-prefix 'FOR-', *þanne* 'THEN', *þaw* 'THOUGH', *no* 'NOR', *ȝut* 'YET', *si/sy* (pret.sg.) 'SAW', *serewe* 'SORROW', *mani(ȝe)* 'MANY'.
48 Specific forms: *hyre* 'HEAR', *a* 'HE', *he* 'SHE', *hire* 'HER', *hy/hi* 'THEY', *fram* 'FROM', *þan* 'THEN' and 'THENCE', *þaw(e)* 'THOUGH', *goud* 'GOOD', *bygunne* 'BEGIN', *no* 'NOR', *ȝulde/ȝild* 'YIELD', *last* 'LEST', *afille* (inf.) 'FELL', *many* (*meny*, *mony*) 'MANY'.
49 Specific forms: *hu(y)re* 'HEAR', *hue* 'SHE', *hure* 'HER', *hus* 'HIS', *þauh* (*þouh*) 'THOUGH', *þanne* 'THEN', *fro/fram* 'FROM', *ȝut* 'YET', *goud* 'GOOD', *þerste/þorst* 'DARED', *forȝute* 'FORGET', *ȝulde* 'YIELD', *meny(e)* 'MANY'.

50 Specific forms: *here* 'HEAR', *þruȝ* 'THROUGH', *fache* 'FETCH', *þauȝ* 'THOUGH', *stude* 'STEAD', *streinþe* 'STRENGTH', *meche* 'MUCH', *afftur* 'AFTER', *latte* 'PREVENT'.

51 Specific forms: *hure* 'HEAR', *-us* (pl. of nouns), *-uþ*, *-un* (verbal endings), *wordle* 'WORLD', *þauȝ* 'THOUGH', *heom*, *heore* 'THEM, THEIR', *nat* 'NOT', *many/meny* 'MANY'.

52 Specific forms: *hyre/huyre* 'HEAR', *hure* 'HER', *gunneþ* (pl.pres.) 'BEGIN', *wordl(e)* 'WORLD', *goud* 'GOOD', *-us* (pl. of nouns), *-ud* past part., *aftur* 'AFTER', *fulde* 'FELLED', *eschte* 'ASKED', *sulf/silue* 'SELF', *þorȝ* 'THROUGH', *nat* 'NOT', *ȝut* 'YET', *swiche* 'SUCH', *meny* 'MANY'.

53 Specific forms: *here* 'HEAR', *he(o)re/hure* 'HER', *heo/sche(o)* 'SHE', *þen(ne)* 'THEN', *ny/neo/no* 'NOR', *sugge* 'SAY', *-en/-o(u)n* pret.pl., *mon* 'MAN', *mony (menye)* 'MANY'.

54 For S Worcestershire features, see p.78 above. The occurrence of *siche* 'SUCH', *thorgh* 'THROUGH', and a high proportion of endings in *-on* suggests a recopying further north in Worcestershire.

55 Specific forms: *here (hure)* 'HEAR', *hure/heore* 'HER', *fram/from*, *aftur* 'AFTER', *þen(ne)* 'THEN', *ȝut* 'YET', *þuder* 'THITHER', *nat* 'NOT', *byȝute* (past part.) 'BEGOT', *mony/meny* 'MANY'.

56 For S Worcestershire features, see p.78 above.

57 For an account of the groupings of the C-MSS, see Donaldson, *The C-Text*, pp.230–1.

58 For the habits of this scribe, see the works quoted in note 45 above. It can be proved from the numerous other MSS that he wrote that, although a West Midlander in origin, he had learned and adopted the form *þerwhiles* from his continuous copying of Gower (see Chapter 6 above).

59 See Skeat's edition of the C-text (Early English Text Society, original series 54: London, 1873), p.1xxiv.

60 Three B-MSS show varying degrees of dialect mixture and indeterminacy, and are not further considered here: C (CUL Dd.i.17), G (CUL Gg.iv.31) and Hm (Huntington, Cal., HM 128). Of these, C is a notoriously layered text which, in any renewed search for relict forms, might repay further study.

61 Specific forms: *huyre* (*hiren*) 'HEAR', *hure* 'HER', *wul* (vb.) 'WILL', *whather* 'WHETHER', *ȝut* (*ȝit*) 'YET', *silf*, *silue* 'SELF', *wurch* (vb.) 'WORK', *thorgh* 'THROUGH', *nat/naught* 'NOT', *mony* 'MANY'.

62 The SW Midland forms are more frequent in some parts of this MS than in others, but they do recur throughout. In particular, the weak preterite in *-ude* suggests Herefordshire.

63 Specific forms: *swych(e)* 'SUCH', *ich* 'EACH', *moche* 'MUCH', *ony* 'ANY', *ffirst* 'FIRST', *ar(n)* 'ARE', *-ende* pres.part., *werse* 'WORSE'.

64 Specific forms: *swich(e)* 'SUCH', *ecchone* 'EACH ONE', *mychil* 'MUCH', *fram* 'FROM', and frequent *e(e)* as reflex of OE *y*, as in *ken* 'KIN', *heer* 'HIRE', *feer* 'FIRE'.

65 Specific forms: *meny* 'MANY', *eny* 'ANY', *myche* 'MUCH', *hit* (beside *it*) 'IT', *ded* 'DID', *þogh* 'THOUGH'.

66 Specific forms: *þeise* 'THESE', *it* 'IT', *iche* 'EACH', *swiche/siche* 'SUCH', *myche* 'MUCH', *lijf* 'LIFE', *þouȝ* 'THOUGH', *þoruȝ* 'THROUGH'.

67 This text is in language very similar to that of the Hengwrt and Ellesmere MSS of *The Canterbury Tales*; cf. Samuels, 'Chaucer's Spelling' (reprinted as chapter 4 above).

68 The Suffolk layer is shown by the minority variants *ich* 'EACH', *michel* 'MUCH', *swiche* 'SUCH', *helde* 'HOLD', *a* 'HAVE', *quatȝ* 'SAID' and *-e-* in forms like

meddel 'MIDDLE', *menstrales* 'MINSTRELS', *Westmenstre*. The stray northernisms include *at* 'TO' (+ inf.), *walde* 'WOULD', *þeire* 'THEIR'.

69 For the localised evidence for these features, see section IV below.

70 Kane and Donaldson, *Piers Plowman B*, p.21.

71 Thus, in both MSS, *any* at II.64, 77, 136, 194, III.313, compared with *eny* at II.200, 201, 207; *ȝif* at II.206, III.111, 118, 135, compared with *if* at II.45, 47, 129, 140, III.7; *com(e)* at II.191, 199, III.35, compared with *cam* at III.110, 178; and *biȝunde* at III.110, compared with *byȝende* at IV.128.

72 Cf. note 39 above.

73 For evidence of provenance, see Sotheby Catalogue of 28 Nov 1967.

74 See N R Ker, *Mediæval Libraries of Great Britain*, 2nd edn., Royal Historical Society: London, 1964, p.150.

75 See Carleton Brown ed., *English Lyrics of the Thirteenth Century*, OUP: Oxford, 1932, pp.xxviii-xxxii.

76 The names of early owners on ff.12v and 23v suggest a provenance not far from Langley Green (west Worcs.), and this is confirmed by a comparison of its language with that of texts from surrounding areas of central and south Worcestershire, Herefordshire and north-west Worcestershire.

77 Chambers, 'The three texts', p.149; for examples of *she* in Langland, see B.II.24, and cf. A.XI.13.

78 Cf. note 16 above.

79 M L Samuels, 'Chaucerian final *-e*', *Notes and Queries* 217, 1972, 445–7 (reprinted as chapter 2 above).

80 In A G Rigg and C Brewer eds, *Piers Plowman: the Z-Version*, Pontifical Institute of Medieval Studies: Toronto, 1983, the editors have proposed that the earlier portion of MS Bodl Bodley 851 contains a version of the poem which antedates the A-version. This question has been excluded from the main account above in order not to confuse the two separate issues of authorship and language. However, the dialect of the Z-version is certainly that of south-west Worcestershire and if this version is accepted as an early work of Langland could quite feasibly be regarded as an earlier and more dialectal form of the language postulated above as authorial. It would then be necessary to assume that some strongly dialectal forms like *ant* 'AND' and *wyt* 'WITH' had been later suppressed, either by Langland himself or by the copyists of the A-, B- and C-versions, and this would have to be taken into account in reconstructing the dialect. A point of special interest is that the Z-version is one of the more strongly dialectal texts (referred to on p.73 above) that either add or omit an initial *h-*, as in *hasket* 'ASKS', *ast* 'HAST', and this both agrees with, and shows the basis of, one of Langland's alliterative practices.

8 SPELLING AND DIALECT IN THE LATE AND POST-MIDDLE ENGLISH PERIODS

M L SAMUELS

In the late fifteenth and early sixteenth centuries, the main obstacle to the localisation of texts on the basis of their dialectal characteristics is a fairly obvious one: the growth of standardisation and the displacement of local usage. The process described by Professor Norman Davis, of writers gradually changing their original regional spellings in the direction of standard,[1] can often be observed as taking place without problem or complication, but nevertheless a large field remains to be explored. J S Gómez Soliño, who is engaged in a wide-ranging survey of texts from the period 1470–1540,[2] has pointed out to me that the process can be seen in the letters of Cardinal Wolsey.[3] In his earlier letters, Wolsey uses forms that derive from his native Ipswich area (*gouyn*, *mych*, *sylf*, *nat*, *leyngth*), but later changes to *geuyn*, *moche*, *selfe*, *not*, *lengthe*. Nevertheless, he retains throughout the typically East Anglian *-gth*, as in *mygth*, *browgth*, *thowgth*, and the accommodation of his own usage to that of Chancery Standard[4] was never completed.

In the wide range of texts of this kind, it is possible to observe two different processes, either separately or combined in the same text:

(i) the writer replaced his own more obviously local forms directly by those of Chancery Standard, e.g. the dialectally peripheral *har*, *ham* or *hor*, *hom*, *mykel* or *mekil*, *sulf* were replaced by the corresponding Chancery forms *their*, *them*, *moche*, *self*;

(ii) the writers replaced his own forms, not by those of Chancery Standard, but by other forms in very widespread use, especially if they were phonetically well suited to function as forms intermediate between dialect and standard, e.g. (for the examples given in (i) above) *her*, *hem*, *myche*, *sylf*.

The result of this second process is a 'colourless' regional language which may present almost as great an obstacle to exact localisation as standardisation proper.

Such changes were not, of course, universal. It is well known that there are dialect survivals in manuscripts of the early sixteenth century, and even in print, if the printer was foreign, a dialectal exemplar's spellings could be preserved intact. A startling example of this is *The Revelation of the Monk of Evesham*, printed in 1482 by William de Machlinia from an exemplar by a scribe whose dialect is sufficiently well preserved in the printed version for it to be localised exactly in NE Worcestershire.

Nevertheless, the influences either towards standardisation or towards a more colourless kind of regional writing are sufficient to render most texts less easily localisable, and, as a result, the correlations that can be made between author and dialect usually depend on other evidence of provenance. The problem here is that the dialectal traits that survive amount to only a small inventory of non-standard forms which, even taken in combination, might belong to a number of widely separated districts: unless the author's place of upbringing is known, we have no means of deciding from which one of these districts the assemblage in fact derives. In the case of Wolsey, for example, S Suffolk is the most likely place for the co-occurrence of *-gth* and *sylf*; but these could also co-occur in a text from N Surrey, so that the question of Wolsey's linguistic provenance could not be settled without a biographical knowledge of his local origins.

In the case of early printed texts, there is the further complication that the printer often preserved some of the author's spellings but replaced others by his own. This may be seen by comparing the printed work of an author like Sir Thomas More with his autograph letters.[5] However, even if no letters survive but the details of the author's provenance are known, it may still be possible to tell which forms are the author's own and which are the printer's, and such correlations can be of importance for editing and textual criticism.

Lastly, there remain texts in which it is impossible to separate two or more scribal strata, or a scribal and a printing stratum. If these are excepted, it should be possible, in theory at least, to classify texts from this period as

A localisable dialect,
B Chancery Standard,
C writing with a regional basis which includes forms from Chancery Standard, and
D 'colourless' regional writing as defined above.

In practice, however, these must be regarded as types rather than hard and fast categories. They can occur in varying combinations, so that some texts have to be graded on a scale, e.g., between A and C, or between C and D.

In the case of type D, there is a further problem of definition. Texts belonging to this type may often give an impression of regional uniformity, e.g. the occurrence of *sylf* in central southern and south-western texts irrespective of whether it descends from M E *silf* or *sulf*; but it is difficult to decide whether such texts can ever be said to qualify for the title of 'regional written standard'. It is reasonable to suppose that they would provide models for local imitation, but no evidence is so far forthcoming of the close imitation that is implied by the term 'standard' in its strict sense. It would probably be a fairer statement of the situation to say that all types except B were normally idiosyncratic.[6]

II

The validity of this theoretical typology will now be tested for two sets of conditions hitherto not considered: (i) unexpected dialect features, and (ii) regionally mixed spelling systems.

As an example of (i), the language of Caxton, the first English printer, will be selected. From the combined evidence of his original prose and translations, many features of his language can be assessed straightforwardly. He maintained throughout certain forms which derive from his Kentish upbringing, like the distinction between *tofore* (preposition) and *afore* (adverb), *hit* (stressed or initial) and *it* (unstressed). For other words, he shows a gradual tendency to discard Kenticisms in favour of standard forms, moving from *axe* to *aske*, and from *thurgh* to *thor(o)ugh* and *thr(o)ugh*.[7] So far, this conforms to the expected pattern of a writer moving from types A to C, and aiming at B; but Caxton's form for 'any' poses a problem, for, although he later admitted as variants the London—and normally Kentish—*eny* and *any*, he uses *ony* throughout, though the Middle English evidence for Kent shows *ony* as a rare by-form only. It was, admittedly, a form that would have been well known, owing to its earlier use in the Central Midland Standard, but Caxton's language contains none of the other identifying features of that type, and that, therefore, seems an unlikely reason for his own use of it. However, the form does occur in certain mid-fifteenth-century local wills in the Kent Archives Office at Maidstone,[8] which, on the grounds of other forms they contain, especially *þe qw(h)ich*, one might at first sight question as being genuinely Kentish at all. The next stage in the argument is to postulate that *ony*, since it is also Caxton's form, cannot be wholly rejected as a late-fifteenth-century Kentish form. The question is, where has it appeared from, and why should it spread just at a time when the language of texts from the south-eastern counties is showing increasing influence from the London standard? The solution is suggested by the other unexpected form, *þe qw(h)ich*. It is tempting to suppose that both this feature and *ony* are signs of E Anglian influence on Kentish, from migration or other connections between the two areas: a likely historical reason for such connections is the wool-trade between E Anglia and its main customers, the Flemings, through the Kentish ports. But the spread of E Anglian forms to Kent need not have been discontinuous: there is some evidence for the spread of *qw(h)-* into Essex earlier in the fifteenth century,[9] and Essex wills[10] from the early sixteenth century show not only *qwhom* but the actual form in question, *ony*. From this evidence it appears that Caxton's use of this unexpected form is due initially to a comparatively recent change in his local dialect, but also to his acceptance of it as a type D feature.

So far, if this view is accepted, the validity of the typology can be regarded as confirmed. Caxton's written language moves gradually from a position midway between types A and C towards type B, but throughout retains a feature belonging to type D. There is, however, a pitfall to be guarded against when features are assigned to different types in this way. In studying the spread of a written standard language, there may be a temptation to restrict oneself to a simple question of a monolithically sociolinguistic kind, like 'What forms did this writer adopt for their prestige-value?' But this short cut from written text to target written language, without consideration of the spoken language, has its dangers. For example, in his earlier prints Caxton uses *them* in stressed, *hem* in unstressed positions. To state that he belongs to type C because of *them* but to type D because of *hem* might not be wholly untrue, but it would certainly be misleading. The development of a system of marked and unmarked forms as stress-variants is a clear indication that they belong in the first instance to the spoken language, and only secondarily to the written. We know very little about the penetration of standard forms into various levels of regional speech in the fifteenth century, but, as I have attempted to show elsewhere,[11] the spread of such systems is due to functional as well as social pressures. A feature of this kind, therefore, must be assessed separately and differently from the rest. It reminds us that the spoken language cannot simply be by-passed, and that any conclusions we reach regarding the written language of the past are always liable to revision if a provable feature of the spoken language has been overlooked.

III

The typology thus survives the first test with a caveat. Its second test comes when we attempt to classify spelling systems which, though internally consistent, combine forms which we would normally regard as belonging to two or more different places. For these systems we cannot assume, as for types C and D, a single regional basis with subsequent changes during a writer's lifetime. The basis here seems rather to be a greater degree of dialectal eclecticism, operating earlier in the writer's life and affecting the formation, rather than the later development, of his individual spelling system. Examples occur in the Paston Letters, now available in Professor Davis's monumentally thorough and scholarly edition.[12] The spelling systems of many of the writers in this collection do in fact tally fairly closely with the dialect of some single place (whether at Paston or elsewhere)[13] and this group includes two members of the Paston Family, John Paston III and Clement Paston, as well as most of those acting as amanuenses. But most of the more educated writers, insofar as they do not, like William Paston I, belong to types C and D,[14] show mixtures of East Anglian spellings that cannot be reconciled with the dialects of single places. This applies, in varying degrees, to John Paston I and II, William II and Edmond II. In all these, there seems to be a basis of N Norfolk spellings and an overlay which is less easily definable but which might sometimes suggest the Norwich area, and at other times Suffolk (Bury or Clare); but the precise assignment of forms to layers is a notoriously difficult task, and the possibility of even some Cambridge spellings cannot be ruled out.

From this it would appear that a provincial education at this period by no means ensured that the student learnt standard spellings. Rather, the spellings he adopted during his formative years would be those of his mentors, or possibly even his peers, at school or university, who would be primarily men from the relevant catchment area—in the case of Cambridge especially Norfolk and Suffolk, and if the spellings came from reading, they would be mainly from books produced locally in the same catchment-areas. Professor Davis, in noting that William II and Clement Paston retained Norfolk spellings in spite of their Cambridge education, has already suggested that Norfolk spellings may have been accepted at Cambridge,[15] and since most university work was presumably still in Latin, it seems likely that, whenever English was used for other purposes, the writers used their own local spellings. What little evidence we have for more elementary teaching in this period, whether in schools or from private tutors, suggests that, where English was used, it was more likely to be some kind of regional English. For example, the handbook of instruction called *The Babees Book*,[16] addressed to children of the 'blood royal', survives in consistent S Suffolk spelling; and it is presumably the result of such instruction that is to be seen in the non-standard spellings used by both Henry VIII and Queen Elizabeth.

Of the many who, in the situation just referred to, were not taught Chancery Standard, some retained their dialect orthography (type A) or modified it later in life (types C and D); and there were doubtless others who were initially taught some variant of types C and D, and retained that, with or without modification. But this leaves a residue of writers whose spelling system was, as a result of various influences to which they had been exposed early in life, not regionally consistent. Such a system can hardly be described any more than negatively, as 'the range of spellings known to, and selected by, a single writer'.

The phenomenon is not necessarily new at this period. There are many texts from the fourteenth and fifteenth centuries which show two or more layers of language, and, although in a majority of them the layers are sufficiently distinct to be attributed to two separate stages of copying, there are a few where the combination suggests a different reason—that a basically homogeneous spelling system has received slight accretions from various neighbouring dialects. A possible example of this is the sermon by John Paunteley on ff. 145r–152v of Bodl Laud Misc 706. Most of its linguistic features will fit exactly at Pauntley in the extreme north of Gloucestershire, on the Worcestershire border, but there is a sprinkling of forms normally associated with the Hereford area (*efter*, *oune*, *dode* 'did', *churge* 'church'), and one other feature (initial *qw-* for *wh-*), the nearest source of which is the nearby Forest of Dean area. On this kind of evidence, one is reluctant to postulate two additional layers of copying when they are more simply interpreted as accretions in the spelling system of a single writer.

It is not immediately obvious why this process became so much commoner at the end of the Middle English period; but it is reasonable to suppose that the growth of *centres* of education (especially grammar schools) caused the breakdown of the minute regional variations of spelling which are found earlier in Middle English and which had presumably been based on the parish. Increasingly, teachers would be employed in areas different from those of their upbringing; their pupils, in turn, would inherit spelling systems which were regionally mixed, and, especially if they became teachers, propagate such mixtures. But whatever the origins of the process, the significance of the development for sixteenth-century spelling practice should not be underestimated, as it is relevant for a more familiar problem: that variants which in Middle English have a precise regional delimitation can recur in sixteenth-century texts as mere 'common currency', without any such delimitation. For some of these, of course, there is the simple and valid explanation that the increase shows the spread of phonetic changes like *er* > *ar* as in *harde* 'heard' and *sarve* 'serve', or added *w-* as in *whot* 'hot' and *whome* 'home'. Then, for printed texts, one may speculate on the possibility that the printer employed a compositor from one of the delimited Middle English areas in question; but such hypotheses are rarely supported by any further evidence, and it seems much more likely that the explanation lies in an extension of the process already described: spellings which have hitherto been members of regional systems become like the coins when two currencies are combined; they have the same functional value as before, but they pass from writer to writer, or from writer to printer and back again, and their regional significance is lost.

IV

If the above arguments are accepted, our list must be extended to include a type E: spelling systems containing mixtures of regional spellings. But even so, many problems remain. An example of particular difficulty is presented by the *Cely Letters*.[17] The Celys appear, from the meagre evidence available, to have been a London family,[18] but much of their correspondence gives at least the appearance of being in a mixed language which is difficult to assess. Only one correspondent belongs with any certainty to type A—William Maryon, whose language can be localised in N Sussex. It is also thought that the northernisms in the language of the younger Richard Cely are due to an earlier sojourn in the north,[19] and a few of William's forms like *aburdde* 'aboard', *mekyll*, and *wrate* 'wrote' seem to demand the same explanation. But apart from this, all the main correspondents (William, George, the two Richards, and Thomas Kesten) write a language which is possibly London in basis, but shows a sprinkling of forms which in Middle English would be associated with Sussex, Surrey or Kent (*har* 'her', *ar* 'or', *theke* 'the same', *fryst* 'first').[20] But such features could be imported into London at any time, and the question to be decided is, therefore: does this language belong to type E, and are its forms merely collections of those in common currency among merchants trading between London and Calais, many of whom would, like William Maryon, have originated in the south-eastern counties? Or, alternatively, could this apparent mixture reflect a spoken London class-dialect for which we have no other evidence, and therefore belong, partly at least, to type A?

In order to proceed with this problem, we are forced to consider a much larger one which is present throughout the Middle English period and becomes more acute at the end of the fifteenth century. Can any of our surviving written records be said to represent a 'City English' as distinct from Chancery Standard? Earlier Middle English scholarship had always assumed a Westminster-City dichotomy,[21] but the textual evidence from the late fourteenth century suggests merely that one type of language, Type III or 'Chaucerian', was then replacing the older Type II or 'Auchinleck' language.[22] For what it is worth, we may note that the older Type II is Essex in basis with accretions from Norfolk and Suffolk, and historically might be nearer to what we would expect for a City dialect. Then, since both Chaucer and Hoccleve had connections with the civil service, we might expect to be able to align Type III with Type IV on the 'Chancery' side of the dichotomy, and oppose them both to Type II ('City'). But there are difficulties in this, for Type III is nearer in language to the late-fourteenth-century Guild returns[23] than to Chancery Standard, and the Guild returns are preferably to be regarded as 'City' even though they differ from Type II. Overall, therefore, the evidence of the late fourteenth and early fifteenth centuries will not fit the traditional dichotomy, but falls naturally into a tripartite division in which Type III occupies a position roughly intermediate between Types II and IV. The salient point for the historian of written Standard English is that each has its own period of prominence, and that these periods are consecutive; but whereas the evolution of written Standard English from this succession of types is reasonably clear, the history of the spoken London dialects of the time is by no means so.

Recent sociolinguistic research has tended to stress the heterogeneity of all—and especially urban—linguistic systems,[24] and varieties of spoken City dialect, differing in some respects from written Chancery Standard, must certainly have existed. The problem is: what evidence of them can be expected in written form, in the face of the growing written Standard? It is often tempting to suppose that early fifteenth-century documents[25] which were written in London but show differences from Chancery Standard must represent a distinct City dialect. But the differences are rarely of more than a few forms which (we would otherwise say) are typical of Essex, Surrey, Middlesex or Herts. Who can tell whether such documents were written by immigrants (or the sons of immigrants) from the Home Counties, or whether they really represent a city dialect which was founded on an amalgam of the Home Counties dialects?

This question has recently been discussed by Professor J H Fisher,[26] and he finds too much variation in non-Chancery London texts of the fifteeth-century to allow the assumption of an established written form of City English. Of the texts he discusses, The Brewer's First Book[27] contains the nearest to the kind of Home-Counties amalgam that might be expected. It has the older South-Eastern *þurgh* and *dede* 'did', Eastern and Southern *on-* 'un-', *e* for usual *i* as in *wendowe* 'window', *kechon* 'kitchen', Eastern and Middlesex *ȝoven* 'given', and the Surrey or Suffolk *frist* 'first'. But this particular combination does not recur, and cannot be proved to be any more than idiosyncratic.

In the late fifteenth and early sixteenth centuries, the situation is similar. At one end of the scale, there is the writing of men known to be Londoners, who deviate only a little from Standard, e.g. Sir Thomas More, in his letters,[28] writes *hit* slightly more often than *it*, *myche* (not *muche* or *moche*), *thorow* (not *through*), and *awne* 'own'. *The Statutes of the Realm 1496–7*[29] show mainly Chancery forms, but also show *myche*, this time with *nat* 'not' and *ayenst(e)* 'against'. It is perhaps significant that *myche* is common to both, and that it is also William Cely's main form. But there the similarity ends, for William Cely also writes *iche*, *yche* 'each', *meny*, *wull*, 'will', *wuld* 'would', *theke* 'the same'. These forms bear no relation to those of other London texts; if we are to judge William Cely's language purely from contemporary evidence, the original question whether he is to be classed in type A or type E remains unanswered. However, if the Cely Letters are considered collectively and compared with much earlier evidence, they turn out to contain some curious echoes of the old fourteenth-century London-Essex type, especially as seen in hand 1 of the Auchinleck MS: Richard Cely Senior's *warled* matches *warld* in Auchinleck, and similarly George Cely's *dede* 'did'; while William and Richard the Younger's *myche*, when considered in the light of Auchinleck *miche* and More's *myche*, suggests that this form might prove to be our main test-word for a connection with City English. If these few correspondences can be trusted, they imply that City English, however fluid as an entity, had some continuity, and that the Cely letters may indeed be classed, at least partly, in type A. How far they also belong to types D and E must remain an open question in view of the uncertain nature of the remaining evidence: sporadic non-standard forms in other London texts of the late fifteenth century like *myche*, *hit*, *nat*, *ayenst*, *thurgh*, *dede*, *youen*. We may conjecture that these constitute the older eastern and south-eastern City elements, as opposed to the more westerly (Middlesex) and Midland Standard forms: but the incidence of such features differs from text to text, and can never be considered more than a slight indication, not proof, of City dialect. The difficulty of deciding the nature of such a dialect is increased when we find that the differences from Chancery Standard may imply a 'Chaucerian' (Type III) rather than an 'Auchinleck' (Type II) basis. For example, the wills of benefactors to the Church of St Mary-at-Hill,[30] which were translated from Latin to English in 1486, have three forms common to both older types (*thurgh*, *thise*, *togider*), but also the typically Chaucerian *nat*. But the main reason for doubt lies in the sheer complexity of the London problem, the fact that it is *multi*dimensional. There are still other texts that are written in a more consistent language than the *Cely Letters*, yet contain only a few more deviations from Standard than texts like Thomas More's letters. The Bodleian MS Gough London 10 (London Chronicle)[31] has the forms *axed* 'asked', *ayenst*, *nat*, *þ(o)urgh (þourow)* and *sleyn* (not *slayn*). If one attempts to localise this text on the Middle English dialect map, it fits best on the border of London and NW Kent. Is this, then, an early manifestation of suburban, as opposed to City, London English? Or is it perhaps the writing of an immigrant from Kent who had succeeded better in rationalising his spelling system than many others of his day? If the latter were true, it could apply also to the putative City texts just mentioned (*mutatis mutandis* for immigrants from Essex, Herts. etc). It is at this point—if not indeed before—that our powers of definition fail us, and we are back in the realm of pure speculation.

As will by now have become evident, the subject discussed here bristles with problems; but when viewed as part of the history of English spelling, it may strike us as merely a transitional stage. By the end of the sixteenth century, most printers were providing an authoritative norm, and private spelling was greatly regularised under its influence.[32] But the editor of a text written or printed during the period under discussion must be prepared to face an extremely complex situation, resulting from a combination of two or more of the following possibilities:

1 The basis of variation may still be regional, and possibly, in large cities, also one of class.
2 The originally regional variants may be combined by writers who have merely 'inherited' or copied them, and hence no longer provide evidence for localisation.
3 There may be a mixture of either 1 or 2—or both—with the printer's system.
4 The printer's system may itself be of the mixed type as in 2, or normative.

NOTES

1 N Davis, 'A scribal problem in the Paston Letters', *English and Germanic Studies* 4, 1951–2, 31–64, and 'A Paston hand', *Review of English Studies*, new series 3, 1952, 209–21.

2 The title of his thesis, presented to the University of Oviedo in 1984, is *Variación y estandarización en el Inglés moderno temprano 1470–1540.* I am indebted to Dr Gómez Soliño for certain of the details given here, and for the orientation gained from his textual analyses.

3 *State Papers, Henry VIII*, Record Commission: London, 1830, Vol I, nos. 134, 161, 183–194, 197–199, 202; P.S. and H M Allen eds, *Letters of Richard Fox, 1486–1527*, OUP: Oxford, 1929, nos. 35 and 37.

For the method used in localisation, here and elsewhere in this article, see A McIntosh, 'A new approach to Middle English dialectology', *English Studies* 44, 1963, 1–11 (reprinted in *Middle English Dialectology*, chapter 2), and M Benskin, 'Local archives and Middle English dialects', *Journal of the Society of Archivists* 5, 1977, 500–14; see also *LALME*, Vol I, General Introduction.

4 The following terms will be used here as more fully defined in M L Samuels, 'Some applications of Middle English dialectology', *English Studies* 44, 1963, 81–94 (reprinted in *Middle English Dialectology*, chapter 5):

Type I: the Central Midland Standard, seen typically in Wycliffite material of the late fourteenth and early fifteenth centuries.

Type II: the written language of London from approximately 1340 to 1380, especially as seen in hands 1 and 3 of the Auchinleck MS (National Library of Scotland, Advocates' MS.19.2.1.).

Type III: the language of Chaucer and Hoccleve, as established by a consensus of MSS.

Type IV: Chancery Standard, the language of government documents from about 1430 onwards.

5 E F Rodgers, *The Correspondence of Sir Thomas More*, PUP: Princeton, 1947.

6 For similar statements regarding the late fifteenth century see N Davis, 'Scribal variation in late fifteenth-century English', *Mélanges de linguistique et de philologie Fernand Mossé in memoriam*, Didier: Paris, 1959, 95–103; and for the sixteenth century see A C Baugh and T Cable, *History of the English Language*, RKP: London, 3rd edn, 1978, p.213.

7 When first published, this article also included references to shifts from *thise/thyse* to *these/thees* and from *tha(u)wh* to *thaugh* and *though*. Dr Gómez Soliño (*Variación y estandarización*, pp.467–8) has since shown that Caxton's spellings for 'THESE' do not exhibit a clear pattern. He also shows that for 'THOUGH', *though* is a major variable even in *The Game and Play of Chess* (1474), beside *thowh* and *thaugh*. *Though* certainly becomes the main form in later texts such as *The History of Reynard the Fox* (1481), *The Life of St Winifred* (1484), *The Art to Learn Well to Die* (1490) and *Eneydos* (1490)—all of which are examples of Caxton's own prose-translations. However, *thaugh* etc. persist as minor variables until the 1490s. In sum, the situation with regard to 'THOUGH' is less clear-cut than had earlier been suggested (see Gómez Soliño, *Variación y estandarización*, pp.448–55, 475).

8 Kent Archives Office P.R.C.32/1, f.78r (1454) has *þe qwich, ony* and *eny*; ff. 67r–69 (1446) has *þe quich*; and U.270, T.236/7 (c.1459) has *oney*.

9 *qw(h)-* spellings occur in texts which otherwise show Essex spellings, in MSS Library of Congress 4, Trinity, Cambridge R.14.32 and BL Sloane 442.

10 I Darlington ed., *London Consistory Court Wills, 1492–1547*, London Record Society III: London, 1967.

11 M L Samuels, *Linguistic Evolution*, CUP: Cambridge, 1972, chapter 6.
12 N Davis ed., *Paston Letters and Papers of the Fifteenth Century*, Parts I and II, OUP: Oxford, 1971/1976.
13 The most remarkable of these writers from a dialectal viewpoint is John Wykes, whose language preserves sufficient south-western features of a markedly peripheral kind to localise it with certainty in Devon: *ther* 'DARE', *twochyng* 'TOUCHING', *ʒeate* 'GATE', *thorf* 'THROUGH'. These forms are of a very restricted currency, and are hardly attested at all east of the Somerset border. A further feature, the *-oy-* spelling as in *moyst* 'MOST', is still more revealing, for, when occurring in combination with the features just mentioned, it is found only in SW Devon and Cornwall (cf. *goys* 'GOOSE' in J J Wilkinson ed., *Accounts of Bodmin Church 1496–1472, Camden Miscellany VII*, Camden Society, new series 14: London, 1875.

Wykes nowhere states that his upbringing was different from that of his colleagues in the Paston household, and it is only because the features in question are peripheral that he can be localised with such certainty. In some other respects he belongs to type D, since he uses the colourless *hem* (not *ham*), *w(h)ych* (not *huch*), and *er(r)*, *er(y)n* (not *byth*, *buth* or *beth*). *er* 'ARE' is found as a variant in two MSS with strong Devon characteristics, BL Addl 33758 and Harley 2386, and Wykes' *er(y)n* is therefore of interest as a possible adaptation of *er* in the direction of Norfolk *arn*.
14 William Paston I wrote in the period before Chancery Standard had become fully established. He retained some East Anglian forms (*iche* 'EACH', *werld* 'WORLD', *weel* adv. 'WELL') but can otherwise be classified as type D.
15 N Davis, 'The language of the Pastons', *Proceedings of the British Academy* 40, 1954, 119–44, p.125.
16 F J Furnivall ed., *Early English Meals and Manners*, Early English Text Society original series 32: London, 1868, pp.250–8.
17 A Hanham ed., *The Cely Letters 1472–1488*, Early English Text Society original series 273: Oxford, 1975.
18 Hanham, *Cely Letters*, p.xii.
19 Hanham, *Cely Letters*, pp.xiv and xxiii f.
20 Cf. *LALME*, Vol I, maps 418, 489, 1062.
21 H C Wyld, *A Short History of English*, 3rd edn, Murray: London, 1927, p.140f.; B A Mackenzie, *Contributions to the History of the Early London Dialect*, OUP: Oxford, 1928, *passim*.
22 See Samuels, 'Some applications', p.7f.
23 R W Chambers and M Daunt eds, *A Book of London English 1384–1425*, OUP: Oxford, 1931, pp.41–60.
24 See, for example, W Labov, *The Social Stratification of English in New York City*, Washington Center for Applied Linguistics: Washington D.C., 1966.
25 See Chambers and Daunt, *Book of London English*, pp.195–205 (Ordinances of the Grocers' Company) and pp.209–35 (wills and other documents).
26 J H Fisher, 'Chancery and the emergence of standard written English in the fifteenth century', *Speculum* 52, 1977, 870–99, pp.896–8.
27 Chambers and Daunt, *Book of London English*, pp.141–91.
28 Rodgers, *Correspondence of More*.
29 *Statutes of the Realm*, Record Commission: London, Vol II, 1816.
30 H Littlehales ed., *The Medieval Records of a London City Church 1420–1559*, Early English Text Society original series 125: Oxford, 1904, pp.1–19.
31 R Flenley ed., *Six Town Chronicles of England*, OUP: Oxford, 1911, pp.153–64.
32 D G Scragg, *A History of English Spelling*, MUP: Manchester, 1974, pp.68–71.

9 SPELLING AND TRADITION IN FIFTEENTH-CENTURY COPIES OF GOWER'S *CONFESSIO AMANTIS*

J J SMITH

I

With reference to the manuscripts of Robert of Gloucester's Chronicle, Anne Hudson has written as follows:

> . . . at any given word all the scribal variants of the MSS must go back to a single form in the original, however indirectly; the interest lies in how and where alteration arises, or why no change is made.[1]

Now that the language of Gower has been identified with that of the Fairfax and Stafford MS,[2] we are able to establish an 'archetypal' corpus of forms to which all the corresponding forms of later scribes bear some relationship: either they are retained, or they are modified, or they are replaced. In this study I intend to investigate three aspects of the Gower tradition opened up by this discovery: (a) how far Gowerian forms persist in copies of the *Confessio Amantis* made during the fifteenth and early sixteenth centuries, and what implications this persistence has for contemporary attitudes to the poem; (b) how far the manuscript-tradition was affected by the advance of 'standardised' written English in the course of the late Middle English/early Modern English period; and (c) the relationship between language and textual transmission in the manuscripts of the *Confessio Amantis*. In an Appendix, I give a brief account of the linguistic contents of all known MSS of the *Confessio*.[3]

II

Any student of the language of the *Confessio Amantis* MSS will be struck by how far a number of idiosyncratic 'Gowerian' forms become 'traditional' in the spelling-systems of these MSS. The following table shows the survival of four 'foregrounded' Gowerian forms in the MSS:

(i) syncopated forms of the 3rd sg. pres. indic. verb, e.g. *makþ*;
(ii) *gh*-type spellings for 'OWN' (adj.), e.g. *oghne*, *ogne*, *oughne* etc. (vs. *owene*, *owen* etc);
(iii) present participle endings in *-end(e)*;
(iv) *sih(e)*, *syh(e)* etc for 'SAW' (verb).[4]

In this table the texts are grouped according to date. It gives only a crude indication of the survival of forms. + = present, even as a minor variable, in any hand or hands of a given MS; − = not present in passages analysed; 0 = item

ITEM / TEXT	*sih*, etc	*-ende*, etc	*makþ*, etc	*oghne*, etc
xvl				
Additional 12043	+	+	+	+
Bodmer	+	+	+	+
Bodley 294	+	+	+	+
Bodley 693	+	+	+	−
Bodley 902	+	+	+	+
Bute	+	+	−	+
Christ Church	+	+	+	+
Corpus Oxf. B.67	+	+	+	+
Dd 8.19	+	+	+	−
Egerton 1991	+	+	+	+
Garrett	+	−	−	−
Glasgow	+	+	+	+
Harley 3869	+	+	+	+
St John's Cbg.	+	+	−	−
Laud 609	+	+	−	−
Morgan M.125	+	+	+	+
Morgan M.690	+	+	−	+
Notts. U.L.	−	+	−	+
New College 266	+	+	+	+
Pembroke	−	−	−	−
Plimpton 265	+	+	+	+
Royal 18.c.xxii	+	+	−	+
Stowe	+	+	+	+
Taylor	+	+	+	+
Trinity R.3.2	+	+	−	+
Yale	+	+	−	+
xvl, 2				
Mm 2.21	+	+	+	+
xv2				
Additional 22139	+	+	+	+
Ashmole 35	+	−	−	−
Antiquaries	+	+	−	−
xv mid				
Arundel	+	+	+	+
St Catharine's	−	−	−	−

ITEM / TEXT	*sih*, etc	*-ende*, etc	*makþ*, etc	*oghne*, etc
Egerton 913	+	+	+	+
Folger	+	+	−	+
Harley 3490	+	+	−	+
Harley 7184	+	+	−	+
Lyell	+	+	−	+
Magdalen	+	+	+	+
Rosenbach	−	+	0	−
Selden	+	+	−	−
Sidney Sussex	−	−	−	−
xv3				
New College 326	+	+	−	−
Wadham	−	−	−	−
xv3, 4				
Morgan M.126	+	+	−	+
xv4				
Caxton	+	+	−	−
Chicago	+	−	−	−
xvil				
Hatton	+	+	−	−
xvil, 2				
Berthelette	+	+	−	−
Chetham	+	+	+	−

not available for analysis in passages available. 'xvl' means 'first quarter of fifteenth century', and so on.

The pattern in these MSS—and, even, in the early prints by Caxton and Berthelette—shows that there was a strong orthographic tradition within which the Gower MSS were produced. It seems very unlikely that this idiosyncratic spelling-mixture persists in so many MSS through pure coincidence.

However, in order to make this argument conclusive, I examined the forms for the same set of items in the nearest comparable MS-tradition, that of Chaucer's *The Canterbury Tales*. In the Chaucer Society prints of *The Pardoner's Prologue and Tale*,[5] a text of about the same length as the tranches I analysed in all the *Confessio Amantis* MSS, no Chaucer MS had *sih* 'SAW' or *-end(e)* (present participle). *gh-* type spellings for 'OWN' appeared only in the following texts:

Corpus Christi, Oxford 198
BL Harley 7334
The Duke of Devonshire's MS
Trinity, Cambridge R.3.3

The first two MSS were copied by the well-known 'Scribe D'; I have discussed the origins of this scribe's *oughne*-spellings elsewhere, and it will be discussed further below.[6] The other two MSS contain well-established layers of language localisable in Kent, where *oghne* etc would occur naturally.[7] As for the syncopated verbs, forms such as *comþ* 'COMES' appear only in the following texts:

BL Addl 35286
The Duke of Devonshire's MS
BL Egerton 2726
Huntington Cal., 26 C 9 (the 'Ellesmere' MS)
BL Harley 7334
NL Wales, Peniarth 392 (the 'Hengwrt' MS)
Trinity, Cambridge R.3.3

The syncopated verbs were a minor variable in Chaucer's own language—*comth* (*Pardoner's Tale* line 781) is required by the metre—so it is, in fact, surprising that such forms survive so comparatively infrequently.

Further examination of the *Confessio Amantis* MSS shows that spelling-tradition could be just as strong in features less 'foregrounded' than those I have identified above. We might examine here two forms which seem to have been archetypal in both *Confessio Amantis* and *Canterbury Tales* traditions: *bot* 'BUT' and *s(c)hold(e)* 'SHOULD'. In both cases, the advancing form in the fifteenth century differed from these: *but* and *s(c)huld(e)*.[8] If we include in the totals all MSS containing *bot even as a minor variable*, then about 44 percent of Gowers have *bot* compared with 7 percent of Chaucers. A similar count for 'SHOULD' shows a similar contrast: about 81 percent of Gowers have the form with *-o-*, against approximately 43 percent of Chaucers. Plainly, the force of archetypal tradition fluctuates from item to item; equally plainly, however, the *proportionate* force on the two traditions I have examined remains the same.[9] In other words, the *Confessio Amantis* MSS display a stronger, more continuing pressure from the language of the archetype than do the *Canterbury Tales* MSS.

Why this happened is hard to determine precisely, but there are a number of characteristics of the *Confessio Amantis* MSS and the way the poem was received which at least suggest possible reasons. Both in his lifetime and after his death, Gower's poem seems to have been thought of as an *auctoritas*. The Fairfax and Stafford MSS present an English text surrounded with a Latin gloss and with versified Latin headings—the kind of apparatus normally restricted to authoritative religious or classical texts. It has been suggested that this 'commentary' was a later addition, indicating the respect in which the text was held.[10] Such respect is underlined by the fact that, as Derek Pearsall has pointed out, many of the MSS of the *Confessio* are 'elegantly illuminated—a mark of status very rarely accorded to Chaucer'.[11] And Gower's authoritative status is indicated by Ben Jonson's use of him as a model author in his English *Grammar*, and perhaps even by his appearance as commentator in Shakespeare's *Pericles*.[12] Such things indicate the high standing in which Gower's poem was held—and, moreover, a particular sort of respect. John Burrow has written of Gower that he 'is perhaps the only Middle English writer . . . to whom the later ideal of "correctness" could be applied without embarrassment'.[13] It seems that this authoritative status attached itself even to the archetypal spellings of the Gower tradition.[14]

III

Whether the *Confessio Amantis* MSS show the influence of 'Chancery English', the form of written English advancing during the fifteenth century,[15] is more difficult to determine. Norman Davis has recently emphasised how the processes of standardisation in the written medium in the fifteenth century have to do with choices among a wide range of possible variables: 'Why one or other of these variants has gradually come to be adopted as the approved type can seldom be confidently determined, and we can often do little more than simply observe the way in which each gives ground or is discarded'.[16] The development of standard written English is currently being investigated by Michael Benskin and Arthur Sandved, and it is not yet possible to predict the outcome of their researches.[17] However, some preliminary conclusions can be drawn by making a comparison between the spellings of the *Confessio Amantis* MSS and Michael Samuels' table of 'Chancery Standard' features.[18] Samuels' table, a comparison of 'Chancery' (i.e. post-1430 standardised, not restricted to government documents) forms and those found in the London English of the best Chaucerian MSS[19] is as follows:

Chaucer	post-1430	Chaucer	post-1430
yaf	gaf	hir(e)	theyre, þeir(e),
nat	not		þair(e), her
bot	but	thise	thes(e)
swich(e)	such(e)	thurgh	thorough, þorow(e)
		sholde	shulde

The following table compares these forms with their equivalents in the *Confessio Amantis* tradition.[20] In this table, + = the presence of a 'Chancery' form for the item in question, even as a minor variable in one hand only; − = the non-appearance of such a form anywhere in the portions of text examined; 0 = not available in the portions of text analysed. The table has certain obvious limitations. I do not include results for the items 'SUCH' and 'THESE' for, coincidentally, the forms for these items in the archetypal language of the Gower tradition are identical with the 'Chancery' forms. Similarly, I do not count *her* 'THEIR' as a distinctive 'Chancery' form; again, it is Gowerian. I include *thr*-type forms of 'THROUGH' among the 'Chancery' forms, since it seems to have been a development of the disyllabic type for this item. As before, the MSS are grouped according to date.

ITEM / TEXT	'GAVE'	'NOT'	'BUT'	'THEIR'	'THROUGH'	'SHOULD'
xvl						
Additional 12043	−	+	+	−	+	+
Bodmer	−	+	+	−	−	+
Bodley 294	−	+	+	−	−	+
Bodley 693	−	−	+	−	−	+
Bodley 902	−	+	+	−	−	−
Bute	0	+	+	−	−	+
Christ Church	−	+	+	−	+	+
Corpus Oxf. B.67	−	+	+	−	+	+

ITEM / TEXT	'GAVE'	'NOT'	'BUT'	'THEIR'	'THROUGH'	'SHOULD'
Dd 8.19	0	+	–	0	–	–
Egerton 1991	–	+	+	–	+	+
Garrett	–	+	+	–	+	+
Glasgow	–	+	+	–	–	+
Harley 3869	–	–	–	–	–	–
St John's Cbg.	–	–	–	–	–	–
Laud 609	0	–	+	–	–	+
Morgan M.125	–	+	+	–	–	+
Morgan M.690	0	–	+	–	–	–
Notts. U.L.	–	+	+	–	–	+
New College 266	–	–	–	–	–	–
Pembroke	0	+	+	–	–	+
Plimpton 265	–	+	+	–	+	+
Royal 18.c.xxii	–	+	+	–	+	+
Stowe	–	–	+	–	–	+
Taylor	–	+	+	–	+	+
Trinity R.3.2	–	+	+	–	+	+
Yale	–	+	+	–	–	+
xvl, 2						
Mm 2.21	–	+	+	–	+	–
xv2						
Additional 22139	–	+	+	–	+	+
Ashmole 35	–	+	+	–	+	+
Antiquaries	–	+	+	–	+	+
xv mid						
Arundel	–	+	+	0	–	–
St Catharine's	0	+	+	–	+	+
Egerton 913	0	+	+	–	–	+
Folger	0	+	+	–	+	+
Harley 3490	–	+	+	–	–	–
Harley 7184	–	+	+	–	+	+
Lyell	–	+	+	–	+	+
Magdalen	–	+	+	+	+	+
Rosenbach	–	+	+	–	0	–
Selden	–	+	+	–	–	+
Sidney Sussex	–	–	+	–	–	–
xv3						
New College 326	–	+	+	–	+	+
Wadham	–	+	+	–	–	+
xv3, 4						
Morgan M.126	–	+	+	–	–	+
xv4						
Caxton	–	+	+	+	+	–
Chicago	–	+	+	–	–	+
xvil						
Hatton	–	+	+	+	+	–
xvil, 2						
Berthelette	–	+	+	+	+	+
Chetham	+	+	+	–	+	+

This table indicates that there is some general movement towards forms which Samuels considers characteristic of 'Chancery Standard'. In thirty MSS dating from before the mid fifteenth century, eighty-five '+' symbols appear, an average of 2.8 per MS; in nineteen MSS and early editions from after the mid fifteenth century, sixty-five '+' symbols appear, an average of 3.4 per MS. This, however, is hardly a decisive shift. It is noticeable that, in the forms for 'GAVE', the 'Chancery' form barely appears on the table. In many cases, the 'Chancery' form is a minor variable only; in other places it is a co-variable with Gowerian forms. The figures in the table above can be seen as similarly distorted by the fact that I have not excluded 'dialectal' MSS which coincidentally contain forms also found in Chancery English.[21]

It is perhaps more significant that a large number of the MSS of the *Confessio Amantis* are written in a 'colourless' dialectal mixture, i.e. a mixture of non-standard forms which is not especially dialectally distinctive, the forms in question having a wide distribution in Middle English.[22] Such mixtures have been described as 'colourless regional standards', coming about

> . . . when a writer replaces some or all of his distinctively local forms by equivalents which, although still native to the local or neighbouring dialects, are common currency over a wider area. The result is not a series of well-defined, regional standards . . ., but a continuum in which the local element is muted, and one type shifts almost imperceptibly into another.[23]

The role of this 'colourless' writing in paving the way for the ultimate success of 'Chancery English' has recently been emphasised,[24] and it is in this context that the spellings of many Gower MSS must be viewed.

How such 'colourless mixtures' emerged might be illustrated by examining the MSS produced by the well-known 'Scribe D', who copied or was involved in copying no fewer than seven early-fifteenth-century MSS of the *Confessio Amantis*.[25] Scribe D worked in London, but was an immigrant to the capital from the SW Midlands;[26] the evidence of the language of his MSS is that he was engaged in suppressing his western origins.[27] The reason for this must be that other varieties of English existed which he considered, consciously or unconsciously, superior to that in which he had been brought up. This is indicated most sharply in those non-Gowerian MSS which, in all probability, he copies from SW Midland and south-western exemplars, viz. his texts of Langland's *Piers Plowman* and Trevisa's translation of *Bartholomaeus Anglicus de proprietatibus rerum*.[28] The following tables contrast some forms in D's MSS of Langland and Trevisa with the archetypal forms of these traditions.[29] The forms D uses are much more widespread in later Middle English.[30]

(a) *Trevisa*

ITEM	ARCHETYPE	SCRIBE D
'HE'	he, a	he
'SHE'	hue, heo, a	sche
'WHICH'	w(h)oche, whuch	which(e)
'MANY'	meny(e), many	many
'FROM'	fram, vram	fro(m)
'THOUGH'	þey, þeyȝ	þough

(b) *Langland*

ITEM	ARCHETYPE	SCRIBE D
'IT'	hit	it
'MANY'	meny	many
'SELF'	self, sulf	self
'YET'	ȝut	ȝit

(NB. Sporadic forms and relicts in both these tables have been excluded.) Of course, it is possible that some intermediate scribes between D and the archetypes have removed the more dialectal forms—although there is good evidence that D's exemplars were themselves written in strongly-marked SW Midlands/south-western English.[31] In general, however, the forms used by scribe D in his MSS of Trevisa and Langland are fairly widespread in Middle English, less dialectally 'coloured' than the equivalent forms in the archetypes.

However, it must be emphasised that such 'standardising' pressures were still uncertain in the early fifteenth century, and this is well illustrated when we examine D's treatment of Gower's language. D makes, on the whole, a good job of reproducing many of Gower's idiosyncracies, albeit with certain consistent modifications and with occasional lapses into SW Midland forms.[32] There is evidence, however, that repeated copying of Gower affected D's usage when not copying *Confessio Amantis* MSS, in his copies of the *Canterbury Tales*, *Piers Plowman* and Trevisa.[33] It is noticeable that all the 'Scribe D' forms in the Trevisa and Langland tables above are not only widespread but also Gowerian. Evidently, a 'doctrine of correct usage' existed, consciously or—more probably—unconsciously, in D's mind, but it would seem to be associated with Gower rather than with more general London English. Thus D 'hypercorrects', taking the curious form *oughne* 'OWN' (adj.) into his repertoire through repeated copying of Gower's *Confessio Amantis*, subsequently introducing it into the other traditions he copies—despite the form's restricted dialectal distribution.[34] The pressures for standardisation may be there, but D looks towards an individual, authoritative usage rather than to a more abstract variety of the language.

The evidence of the MSS of the *Confessio Amantis*, therefore, shows that standardisation was hardly a straightforward matter. None of the MSS is written in 'pure' Chancery Standard. Most present a mixture of Gowerian and dialectal forms, and in many cases the dialectalisms are hard to localise precisely.[35] The prominence of such colourless mixtures in this tradition, beside the evidence of scribe D, suggests that the linguistic behaviour of these scribes was similar to that detected by Cecily Clark in Canterbury just after the Norman Conquest: 'scribal practice . . . does not so much directly reflect any linguistic milieu as represent a compromise between various constraints'.[36]

In one respect at least, such confusions open up new avenues of investigation. As indicated, scribes copying the *Confessio Amantis* generally paid a good deal of attention to the minutiae of spelling in their exemplars. It is to issues to do with the textual transmission of the poem that I now wish to turn.

IV

The most recent full account of the textual transmission of the *Confessio Amantis* is that of John Fisher,[37] but what he says is largely based on G C Macaulay's observations over half a century before. A new collation of the MSS, by Derek Pearsall and others, is under way, but as yet no firm new conclusions have been reached.[38] So the starting-point for any discussion of the tradition must be Macaulay's work.

The basic division of the *Confessio Amantis* MSS made by Macaulay was threefold:

> The first recension . . . is that in which the conclusion of the poem contains praises of Richard II as a just and beneficent ruler and a presentation of the book for his acceptance. The second has . . . additional passages of the fifth and seventh books, with a rearrangement of the sixth book . . . while the conclusion of the poem has been rewritten so as to exclude the praises of the king, and in some copies there is also a new preface with dedication to Henry of Lancaster. The third exhibits a return to the form of the first as regards the additional passages, but has the rewritten preface and epilogue.[39]

However, Macaulay also noted further groupings within these three sets of MSS, and he recognised that 'many errors in the text of the first recension appear also in some copies of the second, and even of the third'.[40] He explained such changes in the following way:

> The process by which this was brought about is made clearer by the fact that we have an example of a manuscript which has passed from one group into another partly by erasure and partly by the substitution of leaves, apparently made under the direction of the author. This is MS Fairfax 3 . . . If a new book had to be specially prepared for presentation, the case would be different, and it might then be worth while to incorporate the additional passages with the fully revised and re-dedicated text, as we find was done in the case of the . . . Stafford MS. Another matter which can evidently be explained in the same way is the reappearance in some copies of the second recension of errors which belong to the first. In producing the originals of such manuscripts as these, partially revised copies of the first recension must have been used as the basis, and such errors as had not yet received correction appear in the new edition.[41]

By such arguments Macaulay accounted for the 2nd- and 3rd-recension MSS. In the first recension MSS, he noted evidence of stages of authorial correction and revision, including metrical smoothing, which (in Fisher's words) indicated 'that the manuscripts were copied from three exemplars, or the same exemplar in three stages of correction'.[42] This is, perhaps, an oversimplification of Macaulay's position; the latter was careful to show that further complexities existed, although he was equally careful not to become bogged down in an attempt at explanation which would, given his initial approach, have probably been fruitless.[43]

It seems to me that the linguistic contents of the MSS can throw light on the processes involved here. While investigating the spellings of scribe D's MSS, I found that there was a persistent set of sporadic forms which seemed to be relicts from a 'Northern' layer underlying both the 'recensions' of the *Confessio Amantis* with which Scribe D was involved (i.e. the first and second recensions). In the table on p. 106, I show the readings for these forms not only in D's MSS but also at the same places in the text in MSS considered by Macaulay to be the 'best' representatives of their recensions and sub-groupings (other than those by scribe D). Including D's MSS, these texts are:

First recension (unrevised):
Bodl Bodley 693
Bodl Laud 609
BL Royal 18.c.xxii
BL Egerton 1991 (by scribe D)
Columbia University Libr, NY Plimpton 265 (by scribe D)
Corpus Christi, Oxford B.67 (by scribe D)
Christ Church, Oxford 148 (by scribe D)
First recension (intermediate):
University Libr, Glasgow Hunter S.i.7
Pierpont Morgan Libr, NY M.125
First recension (revised):
St John's, Cambridge B.12. (34)
Bodl Bodley 902 (partly by scribe D)
Second recension (group b):
Trinity, Cambridge R.3.2 (partly by scribe D)
Bodl Bodley 294 (by scribe D)

The sporadic 'Northernisms' I detected in the MSS are: *-ande* as the present participle inflexion, *þ*-type forms for the third person plural possessive pronoun and *mekil*, *mykil* for 'MUCH' (as opposed to *moche*, the Gowerian form). With these forms I include the use of *-us* in *oþus* 'OATHS', *tribus* 'TRIBES' etc, because the distribution of this form suggests that it is to be associated with this element in the language of these MSS. Its presence as part of this 'layer' might just be taken to indicate that this layer of language is not simply 'Northern' but 'North-West Midland'.[44]

These 'North-West Midland' forms do not appear in those 3rd-recension MSS where they would be sufficiently foregrounded. In the Wadham MS, *tribus* 'TRIBES' appears at VIII.136, and '*mykel* (*mekyl* &c.)' appears at II.2251, according to Macaulay's footnotes; but the Wadham MS is not only a North-West Midland text itself, but also the product of a curious textual history which makes it untypical of the 3rd-recension MSS.[45] As regards the 2nd recension, first group, I have found none of these forms in the Stafford MS. I have not been able to check all the readings in the other text in this group, the Sidney Sussex MS, but Macaulay does note that it has *tribus* VIII.136.[46] For Macaulay's '2nd recension (b)', my access for this purpose has been limited to the MSS copied, in whole or in part, by scribe D, viz. Bodley 294 and Trinity R.3.2 respectively.

Features such as *mykel* 'MUCH', *þair* 'THEIR', *tribus* 'TRIBES', *hengande* 'HANGING' (present participle) are not part of the spelling-tradition of the *Confessio Amantis*, as represented by the Fairfax and Stafford MSS. Yet they

line ref \ MS	Royal 18.c.22	Corpus B.67.	Plimpton 265	Christ Church 148	Egerton 1991	Bodley 294	Bodley 693	Laud 609	Glasgow	Morgan M.125	Bodley 902	St John's	Trinity R.3.2
I.1682	-ande	-ande	-ende	-ande	-ande	-ande	-and	-an(*sic*)	-ande	-and	-ende	-yng	-
3025	-ende	-ande	-ende	-ende	-ende	-ende	-end	-ende	-end	-ende	-ende	-ende	-
II.760	-ande	-ande	-ande	-ande	-ande	-ende	-and	-and	-ende	-ende	-ende	-ende	-
2251	mykel	mykel	mykel	moche	mykil	moche	mekyl	mekil	mykel	mykel	mochel	moche	-
III.1969	-ande	-ende	-and	-ende	-ande	-ende	-and	-ande	-ande	-ande	-ende	-ing	-ynge
1994	mykel	mekil	moche	moche	moche	moche	mikel	mekil	mochil	mochel	mochel	mochel	muchel
V.936	-us	-es	-us	-es	-es	-es	-is	-es	-es	-es	-es	-es	-es
2389	her	here	þair	here	here	here	her	þeir	her	here	here	hire	here
2989	-es	-es	-es	-es	-us	-us	-es	-es	-es	-es	-es	-es	-es
VII.4118	-us	-es	-es	-us	-us	-us	*-us*	-us	-us	-us	-es	-es	-es
4593	-es	-es	-es	-es	-es	-es	-is	-us	-es	-es	-es	-es	-es
VIII.136	-es	-es	-es	-us	-us	-es	-us	-es	-es	-es	-es	-es	-us

persistently appear in corresponding places in the text in MSS which show very different forms of that text—so different that Macaulay and Fisher can write in terms of 'recensions' of the poem.

There would seem to be two possible explanations, not mutually exclusive, for this state of affairs. One is that one text, not the Fairfax MS but modified in a way very similar to it, underlies in its various manifestations all the recensions and sub-groups involved. Such a situation can now be paralleled elsewhere in mediaeval English studies, with the MSS of Langland's *Piers Plowman*. In their exhaustive study, George Kane and Talbot Donaldson showed that Langland, when he came to revise the poem into the state we call the 'C-text', chose to take a corrupt MS of the earlier 'B-text' and then, presumably by erasure and substitution of leaves, converted it into the new text he wanted.[47] This kind of process may well have been easier and quicker than a modification of the collection of wax tablets which probably made up the poet's 'foul papers'.[48]

Another hypothesis which might be favoured in the light of recent codicological research may lie in the use of the concept of the 'booklet'.[49] It is possible that exemplar-copies of texts such as the *Confessio Amantis* and the *Canterbury Tales* were not firmly bound, but existed in booklets loose in the workshop; these booklets would be cobbled together for scribes to copy as occasion and the market demanded. No doubt groups of booklets had a tendency to stick together, but disturbance would not be difficult. We can even guess at the kind of circumstances in which such disturbance might arise. Several MSS of the *Canterbury Tales* and the *Confessio Amantis* are written in several hands—presumably in order to speed up production of rush orders.[50] When the exemplars were split up among the contributing scribes, it must have been only too easy to shuffle up those exemplars when they were returned for storage.

It would appear, then, that a 'North-West Midland' exemplar underlies the following of Macaulay's groupings:

First recension, unrevised;
First recension, intermediate;
Second recension (b).

(It may also underlie the Sidney Sussex MS, from Macaulay's 'Second recension, group (a)'.)

V

The purpose of this article has been not only to present findings, but also to suggest avenues for future research. The language of the Gower MSS, other than that of those copied by scribe D, deserves much greater scrutiny than I have been able to devote to it hitherto; and there are strong indications that further insights might be gained into the complexities of the textual transmission of the *Confessio Amantis*.[51] Similar investigations into comparable traditions—those of Chaucer, Hoccleve and Lydgate are obvious candidates—would be equally illuminating for students of these poets as well as historians of the language. It can be argued that the study of orthography should become a key codicological tool, beside palaeography, textual criticism and the skills of the literary and art historian, for the researcher into fifteenth-century Middle English manuscripts.

APPENDIX: Notes on the language of the *Confessio Amantis* MSS

It is not claimed that these notes on the language of the individual MSS of the *Confessio Amantis* are in any way full; complete accounts of the MSS, with proper references, would take too much space, and work remains to be done on several of the texts described here. MSS are classified alphabetically by location and then repository. Textual classification is according to Macaulay; references are given when the text has already been analysed in *LALME*.[52]

1 Cambridge, Pembroke College, MS 307
First recension, unrevised. Gloucestershire/Worcestershire border; possible constraint from Gowerian exemplar. Possible Northern relicts.

2 Cambridge, St Catharine's College, MS 7
First recension, intermediate. Central Norfolk; some Western relicts.

3 Cambridge, St John's College, MS B.12(34)
First recension, revised. North Herefordshire; some Gowerian relicts. (*LALME* LP 7450)

4 Cambridge, Sidney Sussex College, MS Δ.4.1(63)
Second recension, first group. Ely. (*LALME* LP 219)

5 Cambridge, Trinity College, MS R.3.2 (581)
Second recension, second group. Five hands: (a) largely Gowerian; (b) 'Scribe B' (copyist of 'Cecil Fragment' of *Troilus and Criseyde*, Hengwrt and Ellesmere MSS of the *Canterbury Tales*. See Chapter 5 above, and references there cited); (c) largely Gowerian; (d) 'Scribe D' (see accompanying essay); (e) the hand of Thomas Hoccleve, poet. Some Gowerian relicts, but generally as in Hoccleve's copies of his own poetry.

6 Cambridge, University Library, MS Dd 8.19
First recension, unrevised. North Warwickshire, but some Gowerian relicts.

7 Cambridge, University Library, MS Mm 2.21
First recension, revised. Five hands: (a) mixture of West Gloucestershire and Gowerian forms; (b) largely Gowerian; (c) mixture of Gowerian and Northern forms, though second element hard to localise precisely; (d) largely Gowerian, but a few possible Suffolk forms; (e) Suffolk.

8 Chicago, Newberry Library, Case MS + 33.5
First recension, unrevised. SW Midlands, possibly Warwickshire/Worcestershire. Some Gowerian relicts.

9 Geneva, Bibliotheca Bodmeriana, Bodmer MS 178
Third recension. Six hands: (a) Gowerian; (b) largely Gowerian, with some 'colourless' forms; (c) largely Gowerian, with some possible Northernisms; (d) Gowerian; (e) largely Gowerian, with some 'colourless' forms; (f) largely Gowerian, with some 'colourless' forms.

10 Glasgow, University Library, Hunter MS S.i.7
First recension, intermediate; same hand as 26 below. Largely Gowerian, but some 'colourless' forms.

11 London, British Library, Additional MS 12043
Second recension, second group. Largely Gowerian, with some SW Midland forms, probably Herefordshire/Worcestershire.

12 London, British Library, Additional MS 22139
First recension, intermediate. Two main hands: (a) probably Herefordshire, with some Gowerian relicts; (b) probably Worcestershire/Warwickshire, with some Gowerian relicts. A third, correcting hand is probably a Northerner.

13 London, British Library, MS Egerton 913
First recension, revised; fragmentary. Three hands: (a) some Gowerian forms, but largely colourless; (b) largely Gowerian, but some colourless forms; (c) mixture of Gowerian and colourless forms, some possibly East Anglian.

14 London, British Library, MS Egerton 1991
First recension, unrevised. By 'Scribe D'; see accompanying essay.

15 London, British Library, MS Harley 3490
First recension, intermediate. Largely colourless, but some Gowerian relicts.

16 London, British Library, MS Harley 3869
Third recension. *Literatim* copy of 35.

17 London, British Library, MS Harley 7184
Third recension. Mixture of Gowerian and colourless forms.

18 London, British Library, MS Royal 18.c.xxii
First recension, unrevised. Largely Gowerian, but some Buckinghamshire forms. Same hand as Oxford, Brasenose College, MS 9 (*LALME* LP 6710).

19 London, British Library, MS Stowe 950
First recension, intermediate. Possibly Herefordshire. Some Gowerian relicts.

20 London, College of Arms, MS Arundel 45
First recension, unrevised. Mixture of Gowerian and South-West Midland forms.

21 London, Society of Antiquaries, MS 134
First recension, intermediate. Dialectally colourless; some Gowerian relicts.

22 Manchester, Chetham's Library, MS A.6.11 (6696)
First recension, revised (abbreviated version). Lancashire, but some constrained usage; cf. same hand in Glasgow, University Library, MS Hunter V.2.8 (*LALME* LP 23).

23 Olim Mount Stuart, Isle of Bute, Marquess of Bute's MS I.17
First recension, intermediate. Largely Gowerian, but some colourless forms.

24 New Haven, Yale University, Beinecke Library, Osborn Collection MS fa.1
Third recension. Largely Gowerian, but many colourless forms.

25 New York, Columbia University Library, MS Plimpton 265
First recension, unrevised. By 'Scribe D'; see accompanying essay.

26 New York, Pierpont Morgan Library, MS M.125
First recension, intermediate; same hand as 10 above, *qv.*.

27 New York, Pierpont Morgan Library, MS M.126
First recension, unrevised. Hand of Ricardus Franciscus. Largely Gowerian, but some colourless forms.

28 New York, Pierpont Morgan Library, MS M.690
First recension, unrevised. Mixture of Gowerian and South-West Midland (perhaps mid-Worcestershire) forms.

29 Nottingham, University Library, Middleton Collection MS Mi LM 8
Second recension, second group. Mixture of Gowerian and Northern forms.

30 Oxford, Bodleian Library, MS Arch. Selden B.11
First recension, unrevised. Worcestershire scribe copying Northern exemplar; so curious mixture noted by Macaulay. A few possible Gowerian relicts.

31 Oxford, Bodleian Library, MS Ashmole 35
First recension, unrevised. Probably Herefordshire.

32 Oxford, Bodleian Library, MS Bodley 294
Second recension, second group. By scribe D; see accompanying essay.

33 Oxford, Bodleian Library, MS Bodley 693
First recension, unrevised; same hand as 37 below. Mixture of Gowerian and colourless forms.

34 Oxford, Bodleian Library, MS Bodley 902
First recension, revised. Three medieval hands: (a) scribe D; see accompanying essay; (b) Gowerian; (c) generally Gowerian, but some colourless forms.

35 Oxford, Bodleian Library, MS Fairfax 3
Third recension. Gowerian.

36 Oxford, Bodleian Library, MS Hatton 51
Third recension. Copy of Caxton's edition. Mixture of Gowerian and colourless forms.

37 Oxford, Bodleian Library, MS Laud Misc. 609
First recension, unrevised; same hand as 33 above, *qv.*.

38 Oxford, Bodleian Library, MS Lyell 31
Third recension. Mixture of Gowerian and colourless forms.

39 Oxford, Christ Church, MS 148
First recension, unrevised; by scribe D. See accompanying essay.

40 Oxford, Corpus Christi College, MS B.67
First recension, unrevised; by scribe D. See accompanying essay.

41 Oxford, Magdalen College, MS 213
Third recension. Largely colourless, with some Gowerian forms.

42 Oxford, New College, MS 266
Third recension. Largely Gowerian, with some colourless forms.

43 Oxford, New College, MS 326
First recension, revised. Two hands: (a) probably Worcestershire/Warwickshire, but some constrained Gowerian forms; (b) either Gloucestershire/Herefordshire border or, more probably, South Wiltshire.

44 Oxford, Wadham College, MS 13
Third recension. Two hands: (a) Derbyshire (*LALME* LP 581); (b) North-East Staffordshire/Derbyshire border (cf. *LALME* LP 581).

45 Philadelphia, Rosenbach Foundation, MS 1083/29 (368)
First recension, unrevised. I have only had very limited access to a photograph of this MS. Some Gowerian, some non-Gowerian forms.

46 Princeton, University Library, MS Garrett 136
First recension, revised (abbreviated version). North Warwickshire; some Gowerian relicts.

47 Princeton, University Library, Robert H. Taylor MS
Second recension, second group. Full description of this MS awaited, but scribe D wrote fols. 7r–190r. As far as I can judge, text copied by D exhibits similar behaviour to that of his other MSS. See accompanying essay.

48 San Marino, Huntington Library, MS EL 26 A.17 (olim Stafford)
Second recension, first group. Gowerian.

49 Washington D.C., Folger Shakespeare Library, MS Sm.1
Third recension. Largely colourless, although some Gowerian forms.

NOTES

1 A Hudson, 'Tradition and innovation in some Middle English manuscripts', *Review of English Studies*, new series 17, 1966, 359–72.
2 See M L Samuels and J J Smith, 'The language of Gower', *Neuphilologische Mitteilungen* 82, 1981, 294–304 (reprinted as chapter 3 above).
3 Fuller descriptions of the manuscripts will appear in D A Pearsall, J J Griffiths and K D Harris, *A Descriptive Catalogue of the Manuscripts of the Works of John Gower*, Garland: New York, forthcoming. I am greatly indebted to Professor Pearsall and his associates for giving me access to their materials, and also to the libraries concerned.
4 These forms were selected for reasons of space. Many other distinctively 'Gowerian' forms (see note 2 above and reference there cited) are similarly recorded in the MSS.

5 J Zupitza ed., *Specimens of all the accessible unprinted manuscripts of the Canterbury Tales* (Parts I–IV), Chaucer Society: London, 1892, and F J Furnivall ed., *Specimens of all accessible unprinted manuscripts of the Canterbury Tales* (Parts V–IX), Chaucer Society: London, 1898.
6 See chapter 6 above; also pp.102–3.
7 For all the dialect forms and placings, see *LALME*.
8 See M L Samuels, *Linguistic Evolution*, CUP: Cambridge, 1972, p.169.
9 It should be mentioned that the tranches of text examined in the MSS of the *Confessio Amantis* were, apart from those in the MSS copied by scribe D (see note 6 above and references there cited), limited to passages from Books III and VI. Further work on the language of the Gower tradition—and, indeed, on MSS of Chaucer—is planned; see pp.107–8.
10 See J J Griffiths, '*Confessio Amantis*: the poem and its pictures', in A J Minnis ed., *Gower's Confessio Amantis: responses and reassessments*, Brewer: Cambridge, 163–78, pp.174–5.
11 D A Pearsall, *Old English and Middle English Poetry*, RKP: London, 1977, p.208.
12 See J A Burrow, *Medieval Writers and their Work: Middle English Literature and its Background, 1100–1500*, OUP: Oxford, p.120.
13 Burrow, *Medieval Writers*, p.131.
14 For the widespread appearance of Gowerian language in the Gower tradition, see the Appendix.
15 On 'Chancery English' (otherwise known as 'Type IV'), see *LALME* p.27 and references there cited.
16 N Davis, 'The language of two brothers in the fifteenth century', in E G Stanley and D Gray eds, *Five Hundred Years of Words and Sounds: a Festschrift for Eric Dobson*, Brewer: Cambridge, 1983, 23–8, p.23.
17 See A O Sandved, 'Prolegomena to a renewed study of the rise of Standard English', in M Benskin and M L Samuels eds, *So Meny People Longages and Tonges: philological essays in Scots and mediaeval English presented to Angus McIntosh*, MEDP: Edinburgh, 1981, 31–42.
18 See note 8 above.
19 E.g. the Hengwrt and Ellesmere MSS of *The Canterbury Tales*.
20 For reasons of space, the MS-titles in these tables have been abbreviated. Full titles are given in the Appendix.
21 Such as: Garrett, Notts. U.L., Pembroke, Stowe, Additional 22139, Ashmole 35, Arundel, St Catharine's, Selden, Sidney Sussex, New College 326, Wadham, Morgan M.690, Chicago, Chetham.
22 Such as: Egerton 913 (first hand), Harley 3490, Harley 7184, Antiquaries, Bute, Yale, Morgan M.126, Bodley 902 (third hand), Hatton, Lyell, Magdalen, New College 266, Folger.
23 *LALME* Vol I, p.47.
24 *LALME* Vol I, p.47.
25 See note 6 above.
26 See above, Chapter 6.
27 See above, Chapter 6.
28 See above, Chapter 6.
29 These tables are necessarily selective. For a full account, see J J Smith, *Studies in the language of some manuscripts of Gower's Confessio Amantis*, Diss. PhD, Glasgow, 1985, pp.195–215 and *passim*.
30 For the dialectal distribution of these forms, see relevant maps in *LALME*.

31 This is indicated by the evidence of the other hands in the Trevisa MS, and by the clustering of C-texts of *Piers Plowman* in the South-West Midlands. See Smith, *Studies*, chapter 4; also M L Samuels, 'Langland's Dialect', *Medium Ævum* 54, 1985, 232–47 (reprinted as chapter 7 above).
32 For a fuller account, see Smith, *Studies*, pp.243–66; data on pp.582–686.
33 See chapter 6 above, p.60.
34 See chapter 6 above, note 47 and references there cited.
35 Such as Mm 2.21 (third and fourth hands), Chicago etc; see Appendix.
36 C Clark, 'People and languages in post-Conquest Canterbury', *Journal of Medieval History* 2, 1976, 1–33, p.24.
37 J H Fisher, *John Gower: Moral Philosopher and Friend of Chaucer*, Methuen: London, 1965; see also G C Macaulay ed., *The English Works of John Gower*, Early English Text Society extra series 81–2: Oxford, 1900.
38 This project was announced in the *John Gower Society Newsletter* for 1983, and in Griffiths, 'Confessio Amantis: the poem and its pictures', p.163 note.
39 Macaulay, *English Works*, p.cxxviii.
40 Macaulay, *English Works*, p.cxxx.
41 Macaulay, *English Works*, p.cxxx. For accounts of the Fairfax and Stafford MSS, see chapter 3 above.
42 Fisher, *John Gower*, p.117.
43 See, e.g., Macaulay, *English Works*, p.cxxiv: 'The relations of the [second recension (b) group of MSS] with the first recension and with one another are difficult to clear up satisfactorily. . .'
44 See citations in *LALME*. A dot map for *-us* appears in Smith, *Studies*, Vol II, p.746.
45 See Macaulay, *English Works*, pp.clxiii-clxv. For its localisation, see Appendix.
46 Macaulay, *English Works*, p.389 note.
47 See G Kane and E T Donaldson eds, *Piers Plowman: The B-version*, Athlone: London, 1975, chapter 4.
48 Michael Samuels kindly points out to me that there is a problem with this picture of the process of revision in *Piers Plowman*. This is that *no* C-text (except Scribe D's) contains the London relict forms that are to be expected in any B-text (see 'Langland's Dialect', reprinted as chapter 7 above). This might suggest that Langland re-copied the revised text for subsequent copying.
49 For this concept, see A I Doyle and M B Parkes, 'The production of copies of the *Canterbury Tales* and the *Confessio Amantis* in the early fifteenth century', in M B Parkes and A G Watson eds, *Mediæval Scribes, Manuscripts and Libraries: essays presented to N R Ker*, Scolar Press: London, 1978, 163–210, p.191 and esp n. 60.
50 For examples of the *Confessio Amantis* produced in this way, see the Appendix. Examples of *Canterbury Tales* MSS written in several hands are: BL Addl 5140 and 25178; Bodl Bodley 686; the Cardigan MS; BL Egerton 2726; Glasgow, University Libr Hunter U.1.1; *olim* Cheltenham, MS Phillipps 8137; Bodl Rawlinson poet. 149; BL Royal 17 D.xv, Royal 18 c.ii and Sloane 1685.
51 For instance, a change in the language of the St John's Cambridge MS seems to correlate with a change in textual affiliation; see Macaulay, *English Works*, p.cxxxiii.
52 Fuller linguistic notes, and an essay on the language of the *Confessio Amantis*, will appear in Pearsall *et al.*, *A Descriptive Catalogue*.

BIBLIOGRAPHY

The following is a list of all works referred to in this volume. The list is ordered alphabetically by author, except (a) where no author is recorded (e.g. *Statutes of the Realm*), (b) for the *Dictionary of National Biography* and the *Middle English Dictionary*, and (c) for *A Linguistic Atlas of Late Mediaeval English* (*LALME*) and *Middle English Dialectology*. If an essay has been reprinted in *Middle English Dialectology*, this is indicated both here and in the Notes. Essays reprinted in this book are not recorded here (see Table of Contents).

For the reader's convenience, the first occurrence of a reference in the Notes to each chapter is given in full as here, and then by short title if referred to again in the same chapter. *LALME*, *Middle English Dialectology*, the *Dictionary of National Biography* and the *Middle English Dictionary* are again excepted from this treatment, being referred to by abbreviation throughout.

Allen P S and Allen, H M eds, *Letters of Richard Fox 1486–1527,* OUP: Oxford, 1929.
Atkins, J W H ed., *The Owl and the Nightingale*, CUP: Cambridge, 1922.
Baugh, A C, and Cable, T, *History of the English Language*, 3rd edn, RKP: London, 1978.
Bennett, J A W, 'The date of the A-text of *Piers Plowman*', *Publications of the Modern Language Association of America* 58, 1943, 566–72.
Benskin, M, 'Local archives and Middle English dialects', *Journal of the Society of Archivists* 5, 1977, 500–14.
Benskin, M, and Samuels, M L eds, *So meny people longages and tonges: philological essays in Scots and mediaeval English presented to Angus McIntosh*, MEDP: Edinburgh, 1981.
Benskin, M, 'The Middle English Dialect Atlas', in Benskin and Samuels, *So meny people*, xxvii-xli.
Benskin, M, and Laing M, 'Translations and *Michsprachen* in Middle English manuscripts', in Benskin and Samuels, *So meny people*, 55–106.
Blake, N F, *The Textual Tradition of the Canterbury Tales*, Arnold: London, 1985.
Bourcier, G, adapted Clark, C, *An Introduction to the History of the English Language*, Thornes: Cheltenham, 1981.
Brown, C, ed., *English Lyrics of the Thirteenth Century*, OUP: Oxford, 1932.
Bülbring, K D ed., *The Earliest English Prose Psalter*, Early English Text Society original series 97: London, 1891.
Burnley, J D, 'Inflexion in Chaucer's adjectives', *Neuphilologische Mitteilungen* 83, 1982, 169–77.
Burrow, J A, *Penguin Critical Anthologies: Geoffrey Chaucer*, Penguin: Harmondsworth, 1969.

Burrow, J A, *Medieval Writers and their Work: Middle English literature and its background 1100–1500*, OUP: Oxford, 1982.

Chambers, R W, 'The three texts of *Piers Plowman* and their grammatical forms', *Modern Language Review* 14, 1919, 149–51.

Chambers, R W, and Daunt, M, eds, *A Book of London English 1384–1425*, OUP: Oxford, 1931.

Clanchy, M T, *From Memory to Written Record*, Arnold: London, 1979.

Clark C, 'People and languages in post-Conquest Canterbury', *Journal of Medieval History* 2, 1976, 1–33.

Cromie, H, *Ryme-Index to the Ellesmere Manuscript of Chaucer's Canterbury Tales*, Chaucer Society: London, 1875.

Darlington, I, ed., *London Consistory Court Wills 1492–1547*, London Record Society III: London, 1967.

Davies, R T, Review of Robinson, *Chaucer's Prosody*, *Review of English Studies*, new series 23, 1972, 190–92.

Davis, N, 'A scribal problem in the Paston letters', *English and Germanic Studies* 4, 1951–1952, 31–64.

Davis, N, 'A Paston hand', *Review of English Studies*, new series 3, 1952, 209–21.

Davis, N, 'The language of the Pastons', *Proceedings of the British Academy* 40, 1954, 119–144.

Davis, N, 'Scribal variation in late fifteenth-century English', in *Mélanges de linguistique et de philologie Fernand Mossé in memoriam*, Didier: Paris, 1959, 95–103.

Davis N, ed., *Paston Letters and Papers of the Fifteenth Century*, OUP: Oxford, Vol I, 1971, Vol II, 1976.

Davis N, 'The language of two brothers in the fifteenth century', in Stanley and Gray, *Five Hundred Years of Words and Sounds*, 23–8.

Dictionary of National Biography, Smith, Elder & Co.: London, and OUP: Oxford, 1885–.

Dobson, E J, 'Early Modern Standard English', *Transactions of the Philological Society*, 1955, 25–54.

Dobson, E J, *English Pronunciation 1500–1700*, 2nd edn, OUP: Oxford, 1968.

Donaldson, E T, *Piers Plowman: the C-text and its Poet*, Yale UP: New Haven, 1949.

Doyle, A I, and Parkes M B, 'The production of copies of the *Canterbury Tales* and the *Confessio Amantis* in the early fifteenth century', in M B Parkes and A G Watson eds, *Mediæval Scribes, Manuscripts and Libraries: essays presented to N R Ker*, Scolar Press: London, 1978, 163–210.

Doyle, A I, 'University College, Oxford MS 97 and its Relationship to the Simeon Manuscript (British Library Add. 22283)', in Benskin and Samuels, *So meny people*, 265–82.

Elliott, R W V, 'The Langland Country', in Hussey, *Piers Plowman: Critical Approaches*, 226–44.

Fisher, J H, *John Gower: Moral Philosopher and Friend of Chaucer*, Methuen: London, 1965.

Fisher, J H, 'Chancery and the emergence of standard written English in the fifteenth century', *Speculum* 52, 1977, 870–99.

Flenley, R. ed., *Six Town Chronicles of England*, OUP: Oxford, 1911.

Furnivall, F J, ed., *Early English Meals and Manners*, Early English Text Society original series 32: London, 1868.

Furnivall, F J, ed., *The Harleian MS 7334 of the Canterbury Tales*, Chaucer Society: London, 1885.
Furnivall, F J, ed., *Hoccleve's Minor Poems I*, Early English Text Society extra series 61: London, 1892.
Furnivall, F J, ed., *Specimens of all accessible unprinted manuscripts of the Canterbury Tales Parts V–IX*, Chaucer Society: London, 1898.
Goates, M, ed., *The Pepysian Gospel Harmony*, Early English Text Society original series 157: Oxford, 1919.
Gollancz, I, ed., *Hoccleve's Minor Poems II*, Early English Society extra series 73: London, 1897.
Gómez Soliño, J, *Variación y estandarización en el Inglés moderno temprano 1470–1540*, Diss PhD, Oviedo, 1984.
Gray D and Stanley E G, eds., *Middle English Studies presented to Norman Davis*, OUP: Oxford, 1983.
Griffiths, J J, '*Confessio Amantis*: the poem and its pictures', in A J Minnis ed., *Gower's Confessio Amantis: responses and reassessments*, Brewer: Cambridge, 1983, 163–78.
Hamer, R, 'Spellings of the fifteenth-century scribe Ricardus Franciscus', in Stanley and Gray, *Five Hundred Years of Words and Sounds*, 63–73.
Hanham, A, ed., *The Cely Letters 1472–1488*, Early English Text Society original series 273: Oxford, 1975.
Harris, K D, 'John Gower's *Confessio Amantis*: the Virtues of Bad Texts', in Pearsall, *Manuscripts and Readers*, 27–40.
Hudson, A M, 'Tradition and innovation in some Middle English manuscripts', *Review of English Studies*, new series 17, 1966, 359–72.
Hussey, S S, 'Langland's reading of alliterative poetry', *Modern Language Review* 60, 1965, 163–70.
Hussey, S S, ed., *Piers Plowman: Critical Approaches*, Methuen: London, 1969.
Jordan, R, trans Crook, E J, *Handbook of Middle English Grammar: Phonology*, Mouton: The Hague, 1974.
Kaiser, R, *Zur Geographie des mittelenglischen Wortschatzes*, Palaestra 205: Leipzig, 1937.
Kane, G, *Piers Plowman: the Evidence for Authorship*, Athlone: London, 1965.
Kane, G, and Donaldson, E T, eds, *Piers Plowman: the B-version*, Athlone: London, 1975.
Kane, G, 'Music "neither unpleasant nor monotonous"', in P L Heyworth ed., *Mediæval Studies for J A W Bennett*, OUP: Oxford, 1981, 43–63.
Ker, N R, *Mediæval Libraries of Great Britain*, 2nd edn, Royal Historical Society: London, 1964.
Kivimaa, K, 'The pleonastic *that* in relative and interrogative constructions in Chaucer's verse', *Commentationes Humanarum Litterarum* 39.3, Societas Scientiarum Fennica: Helsinki, 1966.
Kivimaa, K, 'Clauses in Chaucer introduced by conjunctions with appended *that*', *Commentationes Humanarum Litterarum* 43.1, Societas Scientiarum Fennica: Helsinki, 1968.
Koch, J, *A detailed comparison of the eight manuscripts of Chaucer's Canterbury Tales*, Chaucer Society: London, 1913.
Labov, W, *The Social Stratification of English in New York City*, Washington Center for Applied Linguistics: Washington D C, 1966.

Laing M, *Studies in the dialect material of mediæval Lincolnshire*, Diss PhD, Edinburgh, 1978.

Laing M, 'Dialectal analysis and linguistically composite texts in Middle English', *Speculum* 63, 1988, 83–103 (reprinted in *Middle English Dialectology*, chapter 13).

LALME: *A Linguistic Atlas of Late Mediæval English*, by A McIntosh, M L Samuels and M Benskin, with the assistance of M Laing and K Williamson, AUP: Aberdeen, 1986.

Littlehales, H, ed., *The Mediæval Records of a London City Church 1420–1559*, Early English Text Society original series 125: Oxford, 1904.

Macaulay, G C, ed., *The English Works of John Gower*, Early English Text Society extra series 81–2: Oxford, 1900.

McIntosh, A, 'A new approach to Middle English dialectology', *English Studies* 44, 1963, 1–11 (reprinted in *Middle English Dialectology*, chapter 2).

McIntosh, A, and Samuels, M L, 'Prolegomena to a study of mediæval Anglo-Irish', *Medium Ævum* 37, 1968, 1–11.

McIntosh, A, 'Word geography in the lexicography of mediæval English', *Annals of the New York Academy of Sciences* 211, 1973, 55–66 (reprinted in *Middle English Dialectology*, chapter 7).

McIntosh, A, 'Towards an inventory of Middle English scribes', *Neuphilologische Mitteilungen* 75, 1974, 602–24 (reprinted in *Middle English Dialectology*, chapter 4).

McIntosh, A, 'Scribal profiles from Middle English texts', *Neuphilologische Mitteilungen* 76, 1975, 218–35 (reprinted in *Middle English Dialectology*, chapter 3).

Mackenzie, B A, *Contributions to the history of the early London dialect*, OUP: Oxford, 1928.

Manly, J M, and Rickert, E, eds, *The Text of the Canterbury Tales*, UCP: Chicago, 1940.

Marshall, I, and Porter, L, *Rime-Index to Chaucer's Minor Poems*, Chaucer Society: London, 1889.

Middle English Dialectology: Essays on some Principles and Problems, by A McIntosh, M L Samuels and M Laing, edited and introduced by M Laing, AUP: Aberdeen, 1988.

Middle English Dictionary, edited by H Kurath, S Kuhn *et al.*, UMP: Ann Arbor, 1953–.

Mustanoja, T, 'Chaucer's Prosody', in B. Rowland ed., *Companion to Chaucer Studies*, rev edn, OUP: Toronto, New York and London, 1978, 65–94.

Oakden, J P, *Alliterative Poetry in Middle English: the dialectal and metrical survey*, MUP: Manchester, 1930.

Påhlsson, J, ed., *The Recluse*, Universitets Årsskrift: Lund, 1911.

Parkes, M B, and Beadle, R, Introduction to the *Poetical Works of Geoffrey Chaucer: a facsimile of Cambridge University Library MS Gg 4.27*, Brewer: Cambridge, 1979–1980.

Pearsall, D A, *Old English and Middle English Poetry*, RKP: London, 1977.

Pearsall, D A, ed., *Piers Plowman: an edition of the C-text*, Arnold: London, 1978.

Pearsall, D A, ed., *Manuscripts and Readers in Fifteenth-Century England*, Brewer: Cambridge, 1983.

Pearsall, D A, Harris K and Griffiths, J J, *A Descriptive Catalogue of the Manuscripts of the Works of John Gower*, Garland: New York, forthcoming.

Price, D J, ed., *The Equatorie of the Planetis*, CUP: Cambridge, 1955.

Pulgram, E, 'French /ə/: statics and dynamics of linguistic subcodes', *Lingua* 10, 1961, 305–25.

Ramsey, R V, 'The Hengwrt and Ellesmere Manuscripts of the *Canterbury Tales*: Different Scribes', *Studies in Bibliography* 35, 1982, 133–54.

Ramsey, R V, 'Palaeography and scribes of shared training', *Studies in the Age of Chaucer* 8, 1986, 107–44.
Reynolds, L D, and Wilson, N G, *Scribes and Scholars: a guide to the transmission of Greek and Latin literature*, 2nd edn, OUP: Oxford, 1974.
Rigg, A G, and Brewer, C, eds, *Piers Plowman: the Z-version*, Pontifical Institute of Mediæval Studies: Toronto, 1983.
Robinson, F N, ed., *The Works of Geoffrey Chaucer*, OUP: Oxford, 1957.
Robinson, I, *Chaucer's Prosody: a study of the Middle English verse tradition*, CUP: Cambridge, 1971.
Rodgers, E F ed., *The Correspondence of Sir Thomas More*, PUP: Princeton, 1947.
Samuels, M L, 'Some applications of Middle English dialectology', *English Studies* 44, 1963, 81–94 (reprinted in *Middle English Dialectology*, chapter 5).
Samuels, M L, *Linguistic Evolution*, CUP: Cambridge, 1972.
Sandved, A O, 'Prolegomena to a renewed study of the rise of Standard English', in Benskin and Samuels, *So meny people*, 31–42.
Scragg, D G, *A History of English Spelling*, MUP: Manchester, 1974.
Skeat, W W ed., *Piers Plowman: the C-text*, Early English Text Society original series 54: London, 1873.
Skeat, W W ed., *The Vision of William concerning Piers the Plowman, in three parallel texts*, OUP: Oxford, 1886.
Skeat, W W, *Rime-Index to Chaucer's Troilus and Criseyde*, Chaucer Society: London, 1892.
Smith J J, 'Linguistic features of some fifteenth-century Middle English manuscripts', in Pearsall, *Manuscripts and Readers*, 104–12.
Smith, J J, *Studies in the language of some manuscripts of Gower's Confessio Amantis*, Diss PhD, Glasgow, 1985.
Smithers, G V, ed., *Kyng Alisaunder*, Early English Text Society original series 227: Oxford, 1947.
Smithers, G V, 'The scansion of *Havelok* and the use of ME *-en* and *-e* in *Havelok* and by Chaucer', in Gray and Stanley, *Middle English Studies*, 195–234.
Stanley, E G ed., *The Owl and the Nightingale*, 2nd edn, MUP: Manchester, 1972.
Stanley, E G, and Gray D eds, *Five Hundred Years of Words and Sounds: a Festschrift for Eric Dobson*, Brewer: Cambridge, 1983.
State Papers, Henry VIII, Record Commission: London, Vol I, 1830.
Statutes of the Realm, Record Commission: London, 1810–1828.
Strang, B M H, *A History of English*, Methuen: London, 1970.
Tatlock, J S P, and Kennedy, A G, *A Concordance to the Complete Works of Geoffrey Chaucer and the Romaunt of the Rose*, Carnegie Institution: Washington D C, 1927.
Wild, F, *Die sprachlichen Eigentümlichkeiten der wichtigeren Chaucer-Handschriften*, Wiener Beiträge zur englischen Philologie 44: Vienna, 1915.
Wilkinson, J J ed., *Accounts of Bodmin Church 1496–1472* (in *Camden Miscellany VII*), Camden Society, new series 14: London, 1875.
Wyld, H C, *A Short History of English*, 3rd edn, Murray: London, 1927.
Zupitza, J, ed., *Specimens of all the accessible unprinted manuscripts of the Canterbury Tales Parts I–IV*, Chaucer Society: London, 1892.

INDEX OF PERSONS

The following is a list of all the persons referred to in the text and notes, except in bibliographical references (for which see Bibliography).

INDEX OF MANUSCRIPTS

Manuscripts are classified alphabetically by location and then by repository.